Bracket Racing

GETTING STARTED • RULES & REGULATIONS
CHASSIS SETUP • DRIVING TECHNIQUES
WINNING STRATEGIES • ENGINE SETUP • SAFETY

TONY SAKKIS

HPBooks

Most HPBooks are available at special quantity discounts for bulk purchases for sales promotions, premiums, fund-raising or educational use. Special books, or book excerpts, can also be created to fit specific needs.

For details, write: Special Markets, The Berkley Publishing Group, 375 Hudson Street, New York, New York 10014.

HPBooks
are published by
The Berkley Publishing Group
A division of Penguin Putnam Inc.
375 Hudson Street
New York, New York 10014
The Penguin Putnam Inc. World Wide Web site address is
http://www.penguinputnam.com

First Edition: August 1997

© 1997 Tony Sakkis
10

Library of Congress Cataloging-in-Publication Data

Sakkis, Tony, 1960–
    Bracket racing / Tony Sakkis. — 1st ed.
       p.   cm.
    ISBN 1-55788-266-5
    1. Drag racing—United States—History. I. Title.
  GV1029.3.S35   1997
  796.72—DC21
                                         96-49858
                                           CIP

Book Design & Production by Bird Studios
Interior photos by the author unless otherwise noted
Cover photo by Michael Lutfy

NOTICE: The information in this book is true and complete to the best of our knowledge. All recommendations on parts and procedures are made without any guarantees on the part of the author or The Berkley Publishing Group. Tampering with, altering, modifying or removing any emissions-control device is a violation of federal law. Author and publisher disclaim all liability incurred in connection with the use of this information.

CONTENTS

ACKNOWLEDGMENTS

I would like to extend my sincere thanks to Georgia Seipel, John Uyeyama, Sean Clark, Ned Wallace, Al Hoffman, Frank Hawley and Roy Hill.

Special thanks to John Gianoli of Reggie Jackson's for putting up with my endless questions and for spending more time at his shop with me than anyone should have.

INTRODUCTION

This is a how-to type of book, and as with any good one, it is designed to provide the knowledge, guidance and advice to help you with a particular task at hand—in this case, how to go bracket racing.

Of all types of motorsports, bracket racing is one that is most accessible to the masses. You can literally run bracket drags with any type of car, truck or motorcycle, provided it meets minimal safety requirements (none so different than what is required by law on the street). There are hundreds of tracks sprinkled throughout the United States. The cost to run is usually around $10, no higher than $25.

My goal was to break down this sport into increments, to put you in the car before you actually pay your fee and go do it yourself. I hope that I will inspire you to a greater level of participation after having read the following pages.

I can set you on the right course, give you some general tips and a detailed explanation of what to expect, but ultimately it will be up to you to take all of this printed theory and apply it to the track. Once there, you must never stop learning or expanding your knowledge. One of the greatest things about bracket racing is that it is one of the easiest forms of motorsport to start in, but one of the hardest to get right. It is also one where you can set your own level according to skill, budget, time and equipment. You can race with a beater, or a $100,000 racer, at 25 seconds or 8 seconds. Your choice, your pace.

What follows then is a primer on the sport, a racing schematic, so to speak, that will get you started. For many, bracket racing is the beginning and end of their racing career, but for others, it is merely a steppingstone. From then on, your imagination and ambition will be your guide. ■

HISTORY

Drag racing has come a long way since Garlits drove his original Swamp Rat I back in 1959. A good street car with a dose of nitrous and the right gearing could get awful close to what Garlits ran on nitro. That's progress. Photo by Jim Philipson.

Drag racing is truly a motorsport for the masses. With beginnings as an outlaw sport where drivers of "hopped-up" street cars would race one another on lonely back roads and main streets alike, the sport appealed to the youth of America—most of whom had very little money. These youngsters and their hopped-up cars—or hot rods as they were dubbed—raced for status and pink slips, but little else.

Curiosity about cars and speed was inspired by an explosion of interest in machines in general. World War Two, with all its new weapons and technology, had spurred a fascination in anything with mov-

Smoke engulfs this pair of sixties-era rails. The way cars developed horsepower and how they got it to the ground was completely backward compared to today's Top Fuelers, but it was a sport of speed and brute force. Photo by Jim Philipson.

ing parts. On a grassroots level, youngsters turned to the great American icon, the automobile. Tinkering with cars became a hobby for disenfranchised youth, and it was as organized as a rowdy mob could be. Races would be suggested on a dare. Or perhaps as a way to settle a score in place of knives and guns. The crowd would convene somewhere on the spur of the moment, race, and afterward blend back into the night. It was a hazardous business and the element of danger

added to the allure.

Responsible racers, who created the first hot rods prior to the war and who organized racing in the mid-40s, could no longer direct the new crowds to the dry lake beds as quickly as youngsters were appearing to drive. At places called Muroc and El Mirage, cars raced one another on the dusty lake beds, a dozen at a time. And as the war adjusted the lives of the average American, so did it change the lives of the drag racers.

Wally Parks, founder of the NHRA in his Ford, one of his first legally run cars. Parks could never have envisioned the long-lived grassroots interest in drag racing, nor the growth of the professional side of the sport. Photo courtesy NHRA.

Muroc became Edwards Air Force Base, and the semi-legitimate races were forced to move.

In 1948 a National Speed Week took place on the salt flats of Bonneville. Drivers who participated in Speed Week were replaced on the illegal strips tenfold by drivers who were inspired by the Utah speed contests. Some couldn't afford to go, some didn't care to go, being content with continuing to race in the streets.

Racing could be done anywhere—illegally, of course. It could be done on frontage roads, or late at night when the highways were deserted. It could be done in town, in broad daylight, lined up and signaled to start by traffic lights on the main drag in town. It was, of course, "drag" racing. At that transitional period, a new organization, the Southern California Timing Association, was just a degree above the lawlessness of the drivers who participated in the illegal races. The SCTA tried desperately to organize racing. To most outsiders, trying to legitimizer drag racing was something akin to organizing drug addiction or looting. To normal folks, it was less a sport than it was an attitude. A bad one.

During the same period—the early fifties—the local drive-in restaurant became the place to be seen. After activities like football games or movies had ended kids

Dick Landy pulls the wheels up big time in this altered wheelbase Dodge. This period of time in the mid- and late sixties saw an explosion of ideas. This car was run in Super Stock, a precursor to the Funny Car. Photo courtesy Jere Alhadeff.

hung out—as they still do. Having a cool car was the ultimate status symbol, and being cool meant being fast and able to race. This predictable sequence of events was an obvious problem for law enforcement. Cars were running wide open through city streets. People got hurt. Other people complained.

An unlikely hero named Bud Coons, a police officer in Southern California, began a crusade which became one of the biggest racing organizations in the United States. Coons became the champion of drag racing not so much as a racer, but as a cop. He saw the wisdom in making racers allies rather than enemies. It seemed to him a more manageable task to help the kids rather than to fight them. A car aficionado himself, he began getting kids involved in racing as an alternative to other more serious pastimes.

Coons began offering "clinics" to kids, getting top mechanics to show them how to

tune carburetors and change advance curves in distributors and other mechanical things that they weren't getting in shop at school. The first clinics was held at a local Chrysler dealer in Pomona.

Almost immediately, juvenile problems on the street, particularly those associated with drag racing, started to decline; complaints were subsiding. People around the country were watching what Southern California was doing with its speed-crazed youth.

Wally Parks, Editor of *Hot Rod Magazine* (which was founded in 1949 and was instrumental in touting organized drag racing), had established the National Hot Rod Association in 1951. The board of directors of the NHRA put together a program where Coons and several racers would travel around the country and speak to clubs and law enforcement people about the merits of

legitimate drag racing.

The gospel according to the NHRA, which was dubbed the Safety Safari Tour, began in 1954, teaching how dragstrips should be set up and the best ways to design safety into the programs. By this time Coons had write-ups from the FBI, which not only endorsed the racing, but laid out guidelines as to how to establish a dragstrip. With the success of Southern California behind him, as well as the blessings of the FBI and nearly every local law enforcement unit in the U.S. with him, Coons began his task of opening up dragstrips across the U.S.

Racers began to get creative, dropping bigger, newer engines into things like Ford Model Ts and other older bodies, and beefing them up. Others were using pre-war V8s in stripped-down street cars, porting and polishing the manifolds, or changing heads, cams and carburetors. Some were using newer cars, body panels stripped off for weight savings, cars down to the frame rails, giving the word "rail" a new meaning. In 1955, Dick Craft drove his V8-powered Mercury to a top speed of 110 mph over the quarter-mile. And his car is usually credited with being the first "rail," although the car was about as streamlined as a motorhome.

In 1957, Emery Cook ran a top speed of 168.85 mph in the quarter-mile—the new established race length. That prompted the National Hot Rod Association to ban nitromethane. But other groups took over the reins. The American Hot Rod Association and the Automobile Timing Association of America took over the chores of sanctioning Top Fuel contests, creating what could be called a multi-party system. The NHRA had effectively shot itself in the foot by banning nitromethane. But its mistake became a boon to drag racers. There were now at least three major drag racing organizations, all competing for fans as well

By 1971, the NHRA and drag racing had expanded enough to include very definite classes for amateurs and pros. The grassroots movement of amateur bracket racing was beginning. Photo courtesy Jere Alhadeff.

Bill "Grumpy" Jenkins was not only a fierce, wily competitor, he was quite a showman as well, and very instrumental in helping the sport of drag racing grow to where it is today. Photo courtesy Jere Alhadeff.

as competitors.

By the mid-fifties, guys like Dick Landy, Grumpy Jenkins, Don Nicholson, Ronnie Sox and Buddy Martin were beginning to make the sport very impressive indeed. Sox and Martin especially had literally changed the face of the sport when they began running regular clinics and began showing up in team uniforms. And in 1966 Nicholson was to change the face of racing forever when he built the first flip-top funny car ever built. The one-piece body was based around a '66 Comet, a tube-frame monster that Nicholson called simply, "a killer car." So dominant was the design that the cars were now too wild to duplicate at home; factories were too far into the sport for an amateur to compete. The NHRA split the factions into four major groups beginning in 1969: Top Fuel, Top Gas, Funny Car, and Pro Stock.

In 1971, the NHRA ended Top Gas competition. With the definition finally of full-bodied cars being segregated between Funny Cars and Pro Stock, the move to the rear engine dragster now made three clear professional drag racing categories. The demarcation is at that time in history where the pros became true pros and the amateurs truly remained in their classes until they decided to make that leap. That would be in the late sixties and early seventies. That left the great amateurs in their own leagues.

From this time on, the late sixties and early seventies, the amateurs had access to the same equipment as the pros, but they competed on a much more local basis. It was also about this time that the wide variety of equipment became obvious and the great equalizer came into existence: the staggered start. Although it had already been utilized as early as the late fifties and early sixties, handicapped starts really proliferated in the late sixties and early seventies. From then on amateur racing had its own boon of sorts, and anyone who had an interest was no longer limited by money and equipment. ■

In the contemporary world of motorsports, cost is almost always an issue in participation. To get out to the track with a competitive car and enough experience behind you to get the job done and win your race, your division, etc., usually takes a great deal of money and a great deal of time. If you also equate time in terms of dollars, it too becomes an expense that most can ill-afford. In many forms of motorsport, he who has the biggest bucks wins, or at least greatly increases the odds.

DRAG RACING DEFINED

Modern drag racing—at least drag racing at the grassroots level—can be an exception. That is, it can be an exception if you choose

Bracket racing is truly a grassroots sport, accessible to anyone with a running set of wheels. Outright speed and performance take a back seat to consistency. Photo by Michael Lutfy.

"A drag race, by definition, is a contest of straight line speed between two drivers in head-to-head competition between two points."

Although there is activity in every part of the track facility, this is where the focus of attention is–on the strip and especially the starting line. It is here where your race will be won or lost because of your reaction time to the green light.

These high school students are funneling their energy into something that will tax their brains and keep them occupied in a safe atmosphere. This car has been entered by a local high school's auto shop students. Talk about hands-on learning.

to keep costs to a minimum. Like anything else, you can also choose to spend gobs of money and, also like anything else, it certainly does not ensure that you will be any more successful. Drag racing has always been a sport of the masses, and to that extent, it still revolves around introducing neophytes and part-time racers to the racetrack. Of course there are the folks who take it to the next level with nitromethane, superchargers and fully dressed-out big blocks, but the original structure, which is to cater to the ordinary Joe, is still alive and well.

A drag race, by definition, is a contest of straight line acceleration between two drivers in head-to-head competition between two points. It begins from a standing start and ends as either or both cars cross the finish line at the other end of the track. The length of track is most often a quarter-mile since that distance has long ago been established as the standard for drag racing. That

Heads-up racing is all about getting to the line first. He who does, wins. Photo by Michael Lutfy.

"The best driver with an extremely slow car will have a very hard time winning a drag race against an inept driver with lots of purchased power."

does not mean that all tracks are a quarter-mile. Some are an eighth-mile, but for the purposes of this book, we will concentrate on quarter-mile dragstrips.

Also by definition, a drag race is won by the fastest car, or the car that gets to the end of the dragstrip first. Simple enough. Except that the car that wins isn't always necessarily the fastest. Human participation plays a role in how fast the car gets there. Two equal cars with unequal drivers makes for a lopsided race; consequently a person in a less competitive car could make up the difference in machinery with a better drive in the race.

Elapsed Time & Reaction Time—We've devoted a whole chapter to the concept of timing, but for now, elapsed time is the time it takes for the car to go from a standing start at the starting line to the finish line, from Point A to Point B. Reaction time is the length of time between the flash of the green light and when the car actually starts to move—which is a function of how quickly the driver reacts to seeing the light. It is the mathematical relationship between these two, which is discussed in Chapter 5, that is the basis for all drag racing.

Heads-Up Racing

Drag racing from one end of the strip to the other, where both drivers leave at the same time and the car that crosses the line first wins, is called "heads-up" racing. Most pro classes are heads-up racing. It's exciting for fans and it promotes technological progress since the drivers are constantly trying to find a way to make their cars faster. Horsepower, and putting it to the ground, are the keys to winning. Equipment, and how it is tuned, is a much more important factor than driver ability.

But grassroots racing doesn't lend itself very well to heads-up racing. Quite often, the expense of being competitive by having the latest, greatest equipment, often puts the heads-up class of racing beyond the budget of the grassroots racer. The person with the most money will have an advantage. The best driver with an extremely slow car will have a very hard time winning a drag race against an inept driver with lots of purchased power. Money will buy bigger and better engines, will buy equipment that puts the power to the pavement better, and will diminish the human factor.

"Consis-tency and accuracy, rather than speed and quickness (two differ-ent con-cepts, by the way) are everything in bracket racing."

A tricked-out small-block Camaro against a Pinto. Who do you think is going to win? Does this look like an even match to you? But that is what "bracket racing," or "ET Handicap Racing," is all about. It doesn't matter how fast the cars running against each other are. Photo by Michael Lutfy

The 10.76 is the "dial-in" time posted by the driver, indicating that this is the time his car is going to run, not faster. The bracket racer determines this time by gauging the consistency of the car and his driving after a series of practice runs. Photo by Michael Lutfy

BRACKET RACING

So what is bracket racing and how does it differ from heads-up drag racing? In bracket drag racing, and only in bracket drag racing, can you literally pick the level of competition at which you wish to compete and then go out and become truly competitive, with a premium on skill rather than who has the best equipment.

In bracket racing, the driver is the key, although the car is not an insignificant part of the equation. How the car is tuned, rather than the amount of power it puts out, is most important, and it is also what makes racing interesting. Consistency and accuracy, rather than speed and quickness (two different concepts, by the way) are everything in bracket racing.

Dialing In

Bracket racing is done essentially against

The slower car is given a headstart equal to the difference in times, or dial-in. Both should theoretically get to the finish line at the same time. Photo by Michael Lutfy.

the clock. Let's face it, all racing is done against the clock. But in drag racing the clock, and the corresponding ET, is used for more than just measuring the race. It's also used to measure driver performance, tuner performance and crew performance (chances are you are all three of these people).

At each bracket race, you are essentially asked to assess the car's performance, your performance as a driver and the track's condition, and then determine an estimated elapsed time within one hundredth of a second.

You are asked to race within your "bracket" of speed. In national classes, this is known as an *index*. You are required to enter a class based on the ability of your automobile and post an ET on the windshield of your car, an ET you will not be below. This is known as *dialing in*. So you are, by definition, racing between two limits: the lower limit (obviously, the lower the ET the quicker the car) set by the class and the upper limit set by yourself and posted on the windshield.

Breaking Out

If you feel your car can put up a 15.00 second time in the quarter-mile on a particular day, and you write that number on your windshield in white shoe polish, you had better not run 14.99 or you will do what is known as "break out." You must not only be consistent, but very aware of the car, your driving style and the track. If on that particular day, the track is just perfect, the air is conducive to power (more on that in Chapter

If one car goes under his dial in, he breaks out and loses. If both guys break out, the one closest to the time wins. In this example, both cars broke out, but the guy in the right lane is the winner because he broke out less. Note the "win light" on the right siide wall. Speed is not the factor here—timing is.

8) and your car is running well, you may need to adjust the dial-in time written on your windshield, or the best run in your life may lose the race.

Who Wins, Who Loses

Remember, you can not run under your index or bracket times set by your class. In this contest, the first car across the line doesn't necessarily win. In fact, if the first man across the line went too fast, breaking out of his posted dial-in or index, the slower driver wins the race. Essentially, the driver who gets the closest to his index without breaking out, and with the fastest reaction time, will win the race. That's why it appeals to so many drivers, because it's so easy to get started but so difficult to get right.

By the way, the adage you'll hear a great deal around the strip is "first or worst." What that means is that the loser of a race of errors on both sides of the center line is the person who has made the mistake first or the person who creates the biggest mistake. For example, if one driver "red-lights," which means

Unlike big-time pro racing (or even the amateur modified classes) you won't need much to get started. A few handy items are all you need to spend a whole weekend racing. That, and a safe car, truck or bike. Photo by Michael Lutfy.

to leave too early before the green light, and the other driver breaks out, the one who red-lighted would lose—he was first. If two people break out, the one who broke out less wins. If, however, you cross the center line, it doesn't matter when you do it, you've lost. That's a big no-no in drag racing.

Getting Started

Bracket racing is truly easy to get started in, at least compared to most forms of racing (autocross being similar). Bracket racing takes nothing but a valid driver's license, a safe car, truck or bike (which will be defined in a few chapters) a few dollars to get inside the track facility, and some minimal safety equipment, depending on the bracket class you will run.

In cold climates, racing usually takes place from about April to October, and you can usually find at least one regular program per week and often two; in warmer climates you can usually find regular programs at the local track from January through November. In addition, you often have special shows or events that either invite specific drivers or is a contest between local racers and traveling pros. More often, drivers are invited by the kind of car they have. For example, Super Chevy Sundays, Mopar Show & Race and Fun Ford shows invite anyone racing their brand of car, be it Chevrolet, Chrysler or Ford, respectively. You too can compete in those events if you wish when you feel you are ready. They are generally well-attended, but are open to the same basic group of people who bracket race (with the caveat that you have their brand of car).

Now how you pick your dial-in number, how you pick your car, how you adjust your machinery and what to look for will be the source of further study, all of which will be revealed in the next few chapters. Just remember that in bracket racing it is completely unnecessary to spend money on performance enhancements for your car, it's not required that you go through a driving

Bracket racing can even be done on a bike, although safety gear is mandatory.

school to race, nor essential that you know everything there is to know before you get down to the track and actually go racing. All that is required is that you have an interest and are willing to try. It is the one exception to the cost and complexity of most forms of racing. It can, of course, also begin a career as a serious drag racer. The skills learned in a bracket drag race are still valuable to people who compete for NHRA's World Championships.

On the other hand, it can all begin and end at bracket racing. There are thousands of people who aspire to do nothing more than bracket drag racing, but there are different levels of commitment. The ultimate stage is the full-on bracket racer, who is devoting a

"...in bracket racing it is completely unnecessary to spend money on performance enhancements for your car, it's not required that you go through a driving school to race, nor essential that you know everything there is to know before you get down to the track and actually go racing."

Up to 600 cars or more show up in Pomona, California, for the bi-weekly Street Legal Drags to bracket race. The cars are varied, in size and performance level. There are hundreds of tracks with similar numbers of competitors. The sport is relatively inexpensive. What are you waiting for? Photo by Michael Lutfy.

great deal of time and money to making himself as well as his car faster. But most people are not at that level and don't aspire to be. If you've picked up this book, you probably aren't that. Not yet anyway. Chances are you're a novice. Perhaps you've raced once or twice before, but the idea is to learn the sport and determine if you wish to take it to the next level.

Most likely, after you've made the decision to take the next step and actually get out and do it, your first reaction will be to want to go faster and to win. God help you when you get bitten by the racing bug.

The bracket racers who have been at it for awhile may count experience as an advantage, but that's all they have because one thing is for

certain: in bracket racing, throwing money at your car does not make you win more. Consistency is the most important thing in bracket drag racing.

In fact, this is one of the universal secrets of all motorsport: consistency is more important than outright speed. Whether you ultimately wish to stay in bracket drags or whether you one day want to be the World Champion Pro Stock driver, consistency is the platform on which performance is built. You may have outright talent, but if you are unable to apply it consistently, it is worthless. Driving technique can be taught; consistency is an inherent characteristic only you can control. ■

THE PLAYING FIELD

3

The assumption would be that you have been to a pro event at some point as a spectator, or hopefully even a bracket race once or twice, but in case that is not true, the entire process from soup to nuts will be described herein.

Because this is an A-to-Z guide to bracket racing, you need to understand some very basic terms and information.

Although you are not starting as a pro, it is probably a good idea to remind you that things will be totally different than what you've probably seen at your track when the big events come around. In bracket racing—at least at your regular weekly programs—things will happen much more quickly than at a National event. There is no unpacking of transporters, no rebuilding of engines between runs, no three days of racing. For most people, the bracket drags involve driving their own cars to the track, painting their index on the window with shoe polish, getting in line, and then driving as quickly as possible down to the end of the strip.

Before you go streaking off to the top end of the track, you need to familiarize yourself with the track facilities, and some of the procedures. Photo by Michael Lutfy.

The pits tend to be a busy place. Watch what you're doing and keep the speed slow. People can get hurt here if you aren't paying attention. Save the burnouts and lead foot for the track. If you don't you'll be leaving quickly.

Drag racing seems to be a very simple thing: you park on the starting line, wait for the light, stomp on the gas when it appears, drive straight ahead for a quarter-mile, and let off somewhere past the finish line.

Well, if you follow basketball, that's like saying pro basketball players just run up and down the court, putting the round ball in the round hoop. Just as basketball is an extremely complex game that involves intense conditioning, complicated defensive strategies, great offense, and so on, drag racing is a sport that requires intense preparation, skill, and strategy as well.

THE RACE FACILITY

So you need to measure the court, so to speak. What is a dragstrip? How big is it? And so forth. The court, so to speak, in drag racing is not just the dragstrip, but the entire complex. Just like the court is not the only thing pro basketball players need to be able to locate, the strip is not the only place you need to know either.

At any track there will be a front gate. It is the main entrance and usually where one pays the fee to enter the premises. Due to the weather, which can obviously spoil the fun, advance registration is usually impossible, so be ready to wait in line. Or better yet, go early. You'll pay your fee to compete as well

as to watch. In most weekly racing programs, you'll be able to drive your car into the same basic area where the drivers are—even if you aren't racing.

Dragstrips in general are surrounded by large expanses of flat pavement. That is usually the rule because anyone who wishes to compete at the strip will need somewhere to park and leave their gear while they're racing. It is also where a great deal of work is done on the cars. In road racing, to avoid confusion drivers call this area the paddock. In drag racing, it's called the pit area or simply "the pits."

The Pit Area

In the pit area you'll see cars up on jackstands, hulks of cars sitting with their major components on the ground next to them, and quite a few cars that look like nothing more than average street cars with shoe polish on the windshield. But they all park in the same basic area, and for the most part they are all there to race.

You may or may not be assigned a space, but chances are it is first-come, first-served for weekly brackets. If you have a choice, you might want to choose a space close to the staging lane area, and near any restrooms, food concessions, etc. Make sure that you are parked in such a way that you don't block someone from getting in or out to the staging area. The pit area is where you do all of the work on your car between sessions. This includes setting tire pressures, tuning, adding weight, changing oil or tires, etc. In fact, this is the only place it is generally allowed, with the exception of adjusting tire pressures in the staging lanes.

The Staging Area

The pit area will empty every so often into what looks like another large parking lot with about twenty lanes of parked cars. This is called the staging area. Various types of cars will wait with one another, grouped in class, until it's time to go up and race.

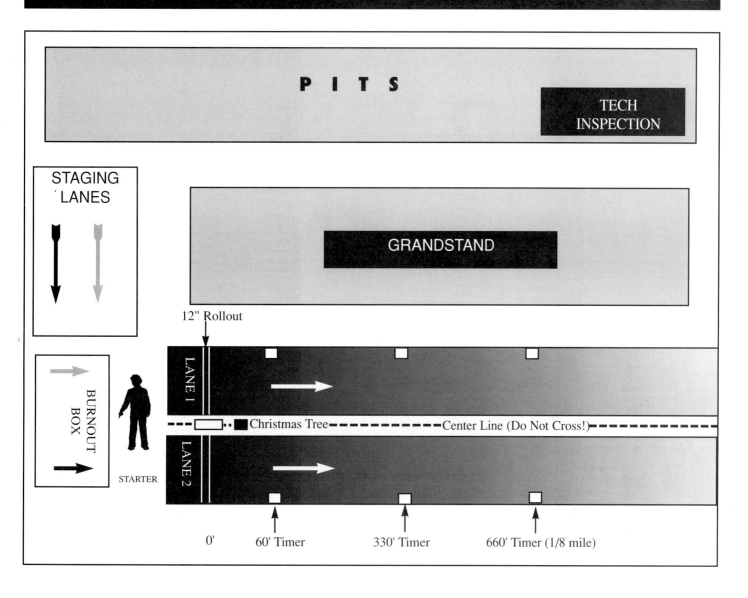

Usually at the rate of two lanes at a time, the cars will advance very slowly forward up to the starter's area, and will eventually race down the track.

The Burnout Box

At the near end of the track, just before the starting lights, is what is called the burnout box or burnout area. The burnout area is used to spin the tires as the car remains in place. The goals are simple: warm the tires for extra adhesion for launching the car, while at the same time cleaning them from any debris and garbage that may have accumulated while driving around the pits. In reality there are some reasons you will not want to do that. These will be covered later,

but for the time being understand that the burnout area is at your disposal for doing just that. You would either use a line lock (see page 41) or a good strong left foot on the brake, get the revs up, and get the rear wheels spinning until tire smoke forms. The car will stay where it is if you've done it right. Once you're finished you will creep forward to the starting line when told by the starter.

The Starting Line

The starting line area is identified easily by the Christmas Tree, a set of lights that will start your timed run. A series of timers will record your time from the first movement of your car until you reach the end of

Just about every dragstrip will have everything you see above. This is the starting line area of the dragstrip. To see the "top end," turn the page. The various timers may or may not be at every track, however. Illustration by Michael Lutfy.

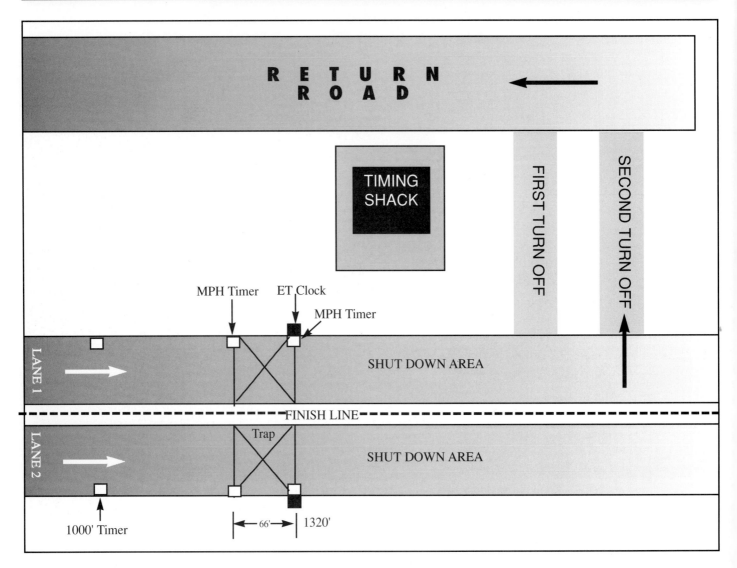

A typical top end. Note that the MPH clocks are located 66 feet before the finish line. There should be two or more turnoffs at each track. Make sure you gradually slow down. Don't make any sudden moves to turn into one of the turnoffs, and if you are in the far lane, check to make sure your competitor in the near lane isn't coming up behind you. Don't make the rookie mistake of turning around and coming back down the dragstrip! It has happened before! Illustration by Michael Lutfy.

the strip (giving you your elapsed time), and from the appearance of the green light (which tells you to go) to the time the car actually moves (which is reaction time).

The Dragstrip

The strip itself consists of two lanes separated with yellow or white center line. *It is imperative that you avoid crossing the center line at all times!*

Although the quarter-mile (1,320 feet) is measured from starting line to finish line, the strip is usually a great deal longer than that because cars need room to slow down once they pass the finish line. This area is called the "shut down area." Some tracks have shut down areas that are as long as 3,000 feet to accommodate 300 mph Top

Fuel cars.

Near the end of the strip itself (strip being the actual 1,320 foot strip of pavement), there will generally be what appears to be two finish lines, 66 feet apart, usually connected with a large "X" (see illustration above). The first line is not the actual finish line, but the line where the top speed clock is started. The second line, is the actual finish line, where both the ET and MPH timers are tripped. The distance between them is known as the "trap." Don't make the mistake of lifting off the throttle at the first line.

Your ET will flash on the scoreboard just past the finish line along with your top speed during practice runs. During the race, the board will show your dial-in on the bottom, and actual time on the top. You will also get a win light (hopefully!) on the scoreboard. If the race was close, there are also little yellow lights some 70-80 feet past the scoreboard, on the top of the wall that tell you what happened—if you won or lost the race. For practice they may or may not be working; if they are connected, then they show who was first through the lights, which is unimportant if you're only trying to get a time to dial-in with. In actual eliminations, they flash on your side if you win, essentially doing the math very quickly to see who was closer to his dial-in. If you break out, or had red-lighted prior to the start, the win light comes on immediately in the other lane. The red-light (only if you leave the starting line too early) will appear back at the Tree and it will also immediately show up on the scoreboard. So if you are given a two-second handicap, and you leave before your opponent, you can tell if he red-lighted or not just by looking at your side of the scoreboard; if the win light is already on, he red-lighted and you won.

Return Road

After you go through the speed trap and gradually slow the car down, there are usually several turnoff exits onto a separate road that runs parallel to the dragstrip called, aptly enough, the *return road*. Prior to your first run, you should check to see how many turnoff exits there are from the dragstrip, and how far apart they are. Usually you'll turn down the return road and disappear behind the grandstands or spectator areas where you'll be deposited directly into the pits. Frequently, like at Pomona, the return road is in front of the stands. That gives the drivers a chance to show off their cars and sponsors to the fans.

Time Slip Booth—Somewhere along the return road there should be a time slip booth, where your run has been recorded and printed out. This is where you collect your time. ■

The return road at Pomona is right in front of the grandstands. During National events, the stands are packed, giving sponsors maximum exposure, and fans a close-up (and slower) look at their favorite drivers and cars. During a weekend bracket race, however, the crowd will look more like this. Observe the speed limit down the return road, no matter how irritated you are about your last run. Photo by Michael Lutfy.

A time slip booth should be located somewhere along the return road. Stop off and get your time slip. The numbers are analyzed in Chapter 5.

YOUR FIRST BRACKET RACE

4

For a few bucks you can be John Force for a day. Just pay the entry fee (anywhere from $10 and up) it takes to get in and then pretend the street car you have is a 5,000 horsepower Funny Car. Plan to get there early, to leave enough time for tech inspection, setup, etc. You don't want to miss the action when the call to staging lanes comes.

Now that you know what to expect, let's take it from the beginning. First, arriving at the track. You'll pay an entrance fee to either race or just watch. Usually it's only a few bucks. It's still a heck of a bargain. You'll usually sign a waiver when you arrive that says you agree not to hold the track responsible for injury or death resulting from any racing incidents. That means whether you are a spectator or a participant, when you pass through those gates you are responsible for your own property and life. Now as a race driver that makes sense, but even as a spectator you have responsibilities. At most tracks the back of the printed ticket clearly states that you can not hold the track liable for being injured even as a spectator. There have been incidents where a car has gone past shut down, plowed through a fence and wrecked parked cars. The track and the driver were absolved of any wrong-doing. Now that's not to say that is always the case. And obviously if you have taken the precautions and are seated in the grand-stands the liability probably rests elsewhere. But you need to be aware that things can go wrong at a race track. Pay attention. Racing is not like football and sitting on the side-lines is not always safe.

You'll want to get to the track early, espe-cially if this is your first time. The pits will be nearly empty if you're an hour or two early, and it will give you time to practice the major task of any drag racer: waiting.

Which brings up a second aspect of rac-ing. A good part of the preparation will be spent on the wait. Make sure you are com-fortable. Probably the first mistake you'll make is undressing or not bringing appro-priate clothing. If it's a night drag, then you've come in jeans and a T-shirt. Once night falls, some places get very cold. Plan ahead. Bring jackets, perhaps a copy of *National Dragster* and something to eat. If you happen to be lucky enough to be there until the end, it could be four, five hours or more before you'll leave. Remember that you'll want to be comfortable. Pack neatly and be prepared for all eventualities. Some dragstrips have snack bars which are open all year; the food sometimes tastes like six-year-old Seven-Eleven food. And some snack bars close for the smaller events and only do business during the big ones. Sorry to have to give you the news, but you aren't participating in a big event. Not yet, anyway.

After you pay your entrance fee, you should receive a schedule of events, rules and regulations, procedures, tech inspection sheet, and various other bits of information to get you through the event. Find your pit space, but remember to keep your speed down. There is almost always a 5 mph speed limit in the pits. Save your speed for the strip, because you could be ejected from the track if you don't obey the speed limit. You

If you're early enough, you may be able to get a good spot close to staging lanes. Make sure that you aren't blocking anyone from getting to the staging area.

take the car off the trailer—or take out the old fast food wrappers and the neckties and tennis shoes out of the back seat—and you're nearly ready to race. Except for tech and your personal equipment check.

BRACKET CLASSES

If this is your first event you'll likely be in the Street class since you haven't modified the car and you're just trying to get the hang of things. It is possible to go into something faster, but for the first time it's suggested you stay with the slower classes. You will usual-ly be with other first timers, and most people will be in cars that tend to be slower as well.

Most beginners are more concerned about the car than they are about driving, which is actually the reverse of what should be

"Most beginners are more concerned about the car than they are about driving, which is actually the reverse of what should be important."

You can go bracket racing in mom's station wagon if you wish. In fact, mom can go racing if she wants!

You probably shouldn't be running a car as powerful as this blown small-block your first time out. Run your daily driver, if need be, just to get a feel for things before you try going 150 mph. Photo by Michael Lutfy.

important. Although this will be discussed in more detail in future chapters, it should be noted that the car should not be a major source of worry at this point. What you're trying to do is to get a feel for the universe of bracket drag racing.

You can go bracket racing with your mom's station wagon if you wish. There needs to be no modification whatsoever. You won't even need a helmet for the slower street cars. This will depend on where you are and under what organizing body, but if you truly do use your mom's stock station wagon, your top speed at the end of the quarter-mile may still be under seventy miles per hour. Enough to have some fun, but not enough to worry about drag chutes or onboard fire extinguishing systems just yet. Although we always recommend that you use a helmet no matter the speed of the car, some sanctioning bodies or local tracks do not require it for cars running under a certain speed and index.

You might consider getting started in something relatively mild. If you have a gas dragster at home you're planning on eventually running as a bracket racer, it might be too much horsepower for your first race. And, if you have a '68 Firebird with a 400 cid stock engine, don't go modifying it. Run the car stock until you've got a handle on where you want to take it. If you really do have a stock Pontiac with a 400, and it's in good shape, the car is worth far more now than it will be once you've finished removing components and replacing them with high-performance gadgetry. You'd probably do better to drive it to work and get yourself an old LTD Wagon to modify.

Remember, the first few events will be to figure out what you want to do in the future. They are information-gathering outings. Treat them as such. You wouldn't choose a major at college without a vague understanding of the different fields of expertise; don't go changing things on your car before you know why you're doing it. Timers and so forth will come later. Just worry about the basics for now.

Before you can race, you need to know what the classes are so you can decide the level you want to race (depending on your car, you may not have a choice). This tends

Here's something you should have picked up before you got to the track, but in case you didn't, they are probably sold there anyway. Most tracks across the country have adopted NHRA's rules and specifications.

to be difficult, since there are enough classes in drag racing bracket competition to suit just about any car. You have to figure which class fits you—and many will fit you for just a few dollars and a few hours of modifications. The idea here is to give you some concept of what you need for just the basic bracket racing classes.

You should already have an NHRA Rulebook, but if you don't, call the NHRA at (818) 914-4761 to get one. The Rulebook is confusing at first. If you turn to the section on classes, you'll find an alphabet soup of nearly 75 pages devoted to car classes, rules specs, safety requirements, and classes based on weight and cubic displacement formulas. But these NHRA class designations pertain mostly to Winston Division Racing series racers. Unless you are competing at this level, you'll need to find the rundown on just six general bracket classes in about half a dozen pages or so. The reason these desig-

"You might consider getting started in something relatively mild. If you have a gas dragster at home you're planning on eventually running as a bracket racer, it might be too much horsepower for your first race."

The High School class is perfect to get you feet wet. It is one of the most popular classes at every bracket race.

nations are so general is that the bracket classes vary from place to place and state to state. What is traditional in one place may not be so somewhere else. And unfortunately, there is no way to give you the differences between regions. What you should do is get a set of rules and class breakdowns from the track where you will be doing the majority of your racing. They will give you a better handle on what you can and can't do and where your car will be running.

I'll use the NHRA's California bracket rules and classes as an example. In some regions this may not work for you, but

because the majority of drag racing is governed by the NHRA, their rules usually are universally accepted.

Categories

There are basically six classes of bracket drag racing: Super Pro (SP), Pro (PRO), Sportsman (SPTS), Street(STR), Motorcycle (MX), and High School (HS).

Sportsman—Sportsman is for cars running 14 seconds or slower. The class runs a 5/10ths full tree and you cannot run electronics, meaning delay boxes and so forth (which, again, you will learn about in Chapter 5). Most of what's on the car will be stock or close to stock equipment, but you will be able to run slick tires in this class, unlike Street class where you must run street tires.

Street—Street, then, is very similar to Sportsman, except that as just mentioned you must run DOT tires. The class uses the full Tree at 5/10ths. The ET breaks are from 12.00 to 24.99 seconds (actually, all the way to 39.99 seconds), which should let just about any car into the club. Anything slower and you should be doing something else anyway. Staging is optional, meaning you can screw up your neighbor's car if you wish by making him wait for you forever (which will not earn you lots of friends). Electronic devices are not allowed.

High School—In High School, you've got basically a wide open class, same ET parameters as Street—12.00 to 24.99. You'll need to run stock mufflers and DOT-approved, or street-legal, tires as well.

Motorcycle—Then there's the Motorcycle class which encompasses every two-wheeled vehicle from 7.50 to 13.99 seconds. You'll be running a 4/10ths pro Tree and need the appropriate safety equipment. Courtesy staging is the rule, which means you can't deep stage.

Super Pro—Super Pro and Pro racers usually will run their cars in this amateur series as well as in the Divisional races for cash

Moving up to pro means laying out a few more dollars for high performance equipment and serious modifications.

and prizes. Most of the time the brackets allow the faster classes to come and test their machinery.

Super Pro machinery is defined by cars which run times between 7.50 and 11.99, which is pretty fast. You shouldn't be here yet, so don't prepare your car for this just now. The series is run with a four-tenths pro light (even though it is an amateur class), and no deep staging is allowed (this is so one won't rev the car and burn out the torque converter while the other guy tries for a psychological advantage ... but this, among other things, will be covered later). Electronic devices (which also will be detailed in later chapters) are legal in this class. Usually, these will be full-on race cars with slicks and big engines, sometimes blown. But no Fuel or alcohol, however. They must run on gasoline.

Pro—Pro class is for cars running 12.00 to 13.99. This is really a major steppingstone class. This will give you a taste of the high

speeds in drag racing, allowing you to modify your car to your heart's desire, but still leaving it street legal. At this point, it's easy enough to turn it into a Super Pro car and then move into National and Divisional event categories like Super Street, Super Gas or Super Comp (all heads-up classes) very quickly. You'll either know you want more or you'll know by this time that you're happy at this level.

When you get into the Super Street, Super Gas and Super Comp Categories you are obligated to run the index mandated by the NHRA for that class. You don't have the flexibility to change your dial-in to suit how your car is running on a given day as in bracket racing.

Say, for instance, that you wish to run a Sportsman car that has been just touching the 12.99 mark. You now believe the car will run faster than that with all the tweaks you've given it, but you don't want to break out. Rather than just pay admission to either

Moving up to NHRA Super Stock or Super Comp classes means having to run the index dictated by the NHRA for that class. The basic principles of bracket racing are the same, but you don't have as much flexibility with your dial in. Photo by Michael Lutfy.

break out or run without going for points, you can go bracket racing. You get to run the car wide open; you can dial-in at, say, a 11.20 and if you can stay at 11.20 or higher you may even win something. It's a competitive way to test new gear.

Local Classes—Recall that most local tracks have their own kinds of regulations as well. They may run their classes dead on what these rules are, and then again they may not care. They may add classes, subtract classes, but essentially, there will always be a class for your car, no matter how slow or fast it is.

Street Car vs. Race Car

So, armed with this information you'll need to determine where you'll run. If this is

your first season, it's recommended that you go the Street or Sportsman route. Don't begin using electronics until you know exactly how the program works. If you like it, move to Pro or Super Pro. Perhaps make that a goal. From there things escalate quickly, both in terms of dollars to be spent as well as commitment. The sport gets more expensive exponentially. Getting 375 or 400 horsepower out of a small block costs you a few thousand, getting it to 600 hp will cost you much, much more. Then of course you have to beef up a great many other parts once the engine is tweaked. So think about this a while before jumping in. As you're considering it, however, take the family car out to the track and race it in one of the slower classes.

Tech inspectors will require that you have a valid driver's license, and that your car be in good running condition. That means that the tires must not have bare cord showing, and all hoses and lines, fuel, transmission, oil, water, brake, etc., be secure and free of leaks. Remove the hub caps for inspection, and make sure you have all lug nuts on. There is much more, depending on class, and each track will have a tech sheet outlining the various requirements.

Tech Inspection

Before you can go tearing off down the track, you'll need to pass tech. This means that a qualified official, a Tech Inspector, will inspect your car to make sure that it is safe and complies with the rules and requirements for the class it will be running. The tech inspection area is usually located about as far away as possible from where you are parked—this is Murphy's Law. Also, keep in mind that everyone must pass tech, and on a typical weekend with 600 cars, that could be a pretty long line. So plan for it.

Before heading over to the area, empty the car of all of the gear you brought—including everything in the trunk. Tech inspectors will poke around, and depending on your class, they will look for specific safety and mechanical items. But in general, common sense applies. They'll check the front end to make sure the wheels are properly secured, and inspect the tires to make sure you don't have any cord sticking out. All fuel, brake, oil and water lines and hoses must be in

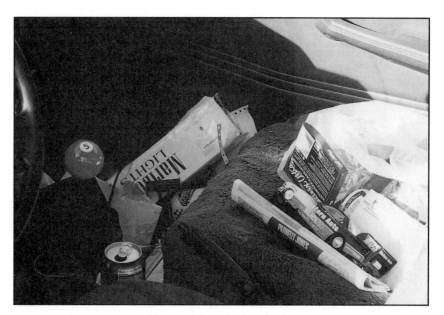

Before you go to tech inspection, empty your interior and trunk of anything that shouldn't be there, or that isn't tied down. Tech inspectors won't pass you if your interior looks like this, and they may send you back to the pit area to empty it out. Then you'll have wait in line again!

good shape, and the battery must be bolted down (no bungee cords, etc.). The tech inspectors aren't going to tear the car down

If everything checks out, the tech inspector will issue a number, and write it and the class in white shoe polish on the windshield. Then it is off to get ready for the call to staging lanes. Photo by Michael Lutfy.

Be ready when the call comes. When you get to the lanes, you may have to wait for a while. A big no-no is to leave your car in the lanes unattended. The line can move forward with little notice. If you hold up the line, you'll become unpopular real quick.

looking for problems, but they will check under the hood, inside, in the trunk and peer underneath. Make sure you aren't dumping oil all over the place.

The tech inspector will sign off on your tech sheet, which, in some cases, you give to the staging lanes director.

YOUR FIRST RUN

The rest of this book goes into more detail on every step of bracket racing from performing a burnout to adjusting dial-in, track tuning, etc. But for now, I'm going to give you an overview on what to expect during a typical run. If you have a chance, you should go and observe a few runs at the starting line to get a feel for the procedure, before jumping into the car.

Staging Lanes

The first thing you'll do is head for the staging lanes when the announcer calls for the cars in your class. At big tracks like Pomona, the announcer is also plugged into an AM radio station, which is easier than trying to catch it on the loudspeakers. He should indicate what lane you are going to be in, so when the call comes, be ready and leave your gear neatly stacked in the pits and head to the staging lanes at the speed limit. It would be wise to ask the guy in front or behind you if he's in the same class, or at least look on his windshield to make sure. It will be less embarrassing if you do this now than if you get all the way up to the starting line.

The next part is easy: just wait for the cars in the other class to finish and eventually the line will start to move. It may be easier just to push your car than to restart it, move twenty feet and then shut it off. You be the judge. In some cases, you'll be waiting for quite a while in the staging lanes. But please don't leave your car. When the line starts to move it moves quickly. If you're gone when your class is called, you'll create a serious

BASIC DRAGSTRIP RULES

1. Obey the starter!
2. Burnouts across the starting line are prohibited unless approved for your class.
3. Do not begin your burnout until the cars have left the starting line, or until you're instructed to do so by an official.
4. Make sure your dial-in number and car number are clearly legible.
5. A crew member should never approach the starter once the cars are staged, nor should he or she argue with the starter during a race.
6. Never drive the opposite direction on the dragstrip.
7. Most tracks enforce a staging courtesy rule: One car cannot fully stage until the other car has lighted the prestage light.
8. Deep staging is not allowed when the blue light on the Tree is lit.
9. If your car breaks, pull off to the side and out of the racing groove immediately.
10. If your car gets crossed-up in the burnout box, stop, straighten the car, and do it again. Do not continue the burnout and risk hitting someone or something.

Reprinted courtesy Hot Rod *magazine*

"For your first run, you may not want to try a burnout just yet. Focus on the start until you get used to things."

log jam and hold things up, and you won't make friends with the guy behind you. When in staging, stay in or around your car.

Eventually, you'll creep forward. Just like the pros, the cars in your class will be lined up in two or more lanes. One car from each lane will be motioned to the burnout area by the staging director, which is usually about fifty feet from the starting line. For your first run, you may not want to try a burnout just yet. Focus on the start until you get used to things. If you insist, however, at least turn to page for the proper technique.

Staging—The cars in front of you have raced to the end of the track and it's now your turn. Wait until you are waved to the line. Remember, this is only a timed practice run, so it won't be the end of the world if you red-light or cut a 1.5 second reaction time. The idea is to get a feel for how your car is performing so you can determine the time you will run for the rest of the weekend.

The staging process consists of tripping a set of light beams with your wheels. There are a pair (or sometimes two pair working together) of lights: one for pre-staging and

You'll be motioned forward to the burnout box by the staging lanes director. At that point, you'll take your cue to burnout (or not) by the burnout box director. At smaller tracks and events, one guy usually performs both jobs. Pay attention, because at this point, things move quickly, and you'll irritate everyone if you hold things up.

Don't even think of playing games here. Wait for the starter to motion you forward, then stage right away by creeping forward enough to light the two sets of amber lights on top of the Tree (this will all make more sense after you read the next chapter). Get ready for the green. Photo by Michael Lutfy.

one for staging. The first light will tell you where you are. It means you have about six inches before the stage light comes on. Staging and strategy will be covered in greater detail in later chapters, but for now, don't mess around. Get up to the line, pre-stage, then creep forward slowly and stage, lighting both amber lights on your side of the Tree. Then prepare for the start.

The lights will blink sequentially down the Tree then go green. This is unlike a pro Tree you may have seen at an event or on TV, where all of them go amber, then green.

Launching—Although we'll get into anticipating the green later, for now, do the best you can and tromp the accelerator, focusing on the strip ahead. However, be aware what the car is doing. Make sure you haven't spun the wheels, and keep the car pointed straight. The launching area is frequently cleaned and inspected by officials after nearly every run, so it should not be wet or slick with oil. Nevertheless, it may still be slightly slippery depending on when the last time it was swept off. You should have the seat-of-the-pants feel for a slipping car, but if you don't there's not a lot of help you can get other than experience. If the car is slipping, the first reaction is to step out of the throttle. Usually a feathering of the pedal will do just fine. Many drivers say that the tires will often slip at some point during the run.

If, during the run, the car starts to get sideways, or tracks from one side to the other, don't be a hero by trying to save the car and the run. Lift off the throttle, get the car square, and abort the run.

In Chapter 11, safety as well as a brief dis-

The finish line will be there before you know it. Lift off slowly and gradually—don't nail the brakes or try to make the first turnoff with a sudden move. Make your way onto the return road, and remember to get your time slip.

Time to make your way back to the pits and assess what just happened. There's plenty to do, as you'll find out in the chapters ahead. Photo by Michael Lutfy.

cussion on car control will be provided, but for now let's assume the car is performing flawlessly and tracking straight and true, as you rip through the lights with a time of 15.010 with a terminal speed of 80. 22 mph.

Shutdown—This is one of the most critical times of the whole run. You've just reached top speed and now it's over—at least as far as timing and scoring is concerned. But you've still got to slow down enough to make the turnoff to the return road. Once you pass the trap lights at the end of the track, don't just jerk your foot off the gas and onto the brakes. Slow the car down progressively—there will be plenty of room. Ease off the throttle, ease onto the brakes. Keep track of your surroundings at this point. Some tracks have foot markers so you know where you are, and there should be more than one turnoff lane. If you're going too fast, don't slam on the brakes to try and make the first one. Take the second or third one instead. Remember how long it takes to slow the car down safely and make a mental note of it for future runs.

Take the turnoff slowly and then drive down the return road at the speed limit, which now seems like a crawl. Whatever you do, do not make the dangerous mistake of turning back down the dragstrip! Although you may think this is absurd, it has actually happened before—more than once. Drivers get so excited (especially rookies) with the thrill of the speed and all that, that they lose their head.

As mentioned, somewhere along the return road, usually just out of harm's way of the finish line, a timing/scoring booth will be set up. Sometimes it might be nothing more than a table. You'll have to stop and pick up your time slip which contains the timing information of your run, such as E.T., R.T. and top speed. In the next chapter, we'll discuss what all of those numbers mean. Don't be surprised if you did poorly in reaction time. You're looking for 0.500; you may have 0.750 or worse. On your first run it's going to be difficult to post wonderful results.

All that's left is to head back to the pits and wait for the next call to the staging lane. You'll want to check the car out; its temperature, pressures and so forth, which will be explained in the chapters ahead. ■

5

TIMING

It's all a matter of timing! Understanding the relationship between elapsed time and reaction time is critical in order for you to be competitive. By the way, the view in this picture is looking back toward the starting line. There are two sets of lights on the Tree, one set facing toward the starting line, the other toward the finish line. Photo by Michael Lutfy.

Before you can be competitive, you need to know the factors that affect your performance. In drag racing in general, timing is everything. Whether at a U.S. National, or a Bracket Night at the local strip, the significance of elapsed time and reaction time, and how they are interrelated, can not be underestimated.

THE CHRISTMAS TREE

Let's take a closer look at the starting Tree itself. The ET as well as the RT is based on the starter's light or, as you may have heard it referred to as "the Christmas Tree," or simply "The Tree."

The Tree will have five lights facing both toward and away from each driver, lined in

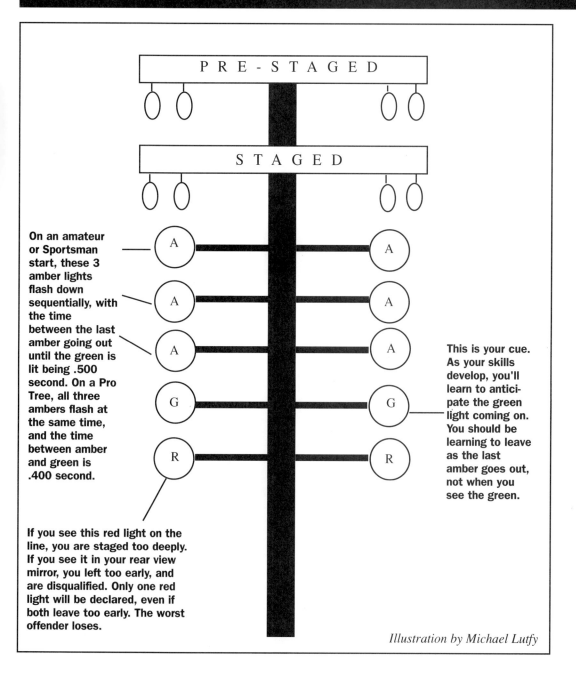

On an amateur or Sportsman start, these 3 amber lights flash down sequentially, with the time between the last amber going out until the green is lit being .500 second. On a Pro Tree, all three ambers flash at the same time, and the time between amber and green is .400 second.

This is your cue. As your skills develop, you'll learn to anticipate the green light coming on. You should be learning to leave as the last amber goes out, not when you see the green.

If you see this red light on the line, you are staged too deeply. If you see it in your rear view mirror, you left too early, and are disqualified. Only one red light will be declared, even if both leave too early. The worst offender loses.

Illustration by Michael Lutfy

a pair of columns (identical columns will be on the opposite side of the Tree so the spectators can see as well). On each column, starting from the top down, there will be three amber lights, one green and a red. In addition, at the top of the Tree is a set of two pre-stage and two stage lights, usually under some sort of sign labeling them as such. A Pro Tree is different from an amateur Tree in that it flashes differently—other than that, they look identical (in fact one Tree is used for both Pro and Sportsman racing). Once staged, the Pro Tree flashes all three amber lights on the Tree at once and then flashes green. An amateur Tree flashes sequentially—top first, then second from the top, and so on until it hits green. At that point the driver should already be under way. The difference between the Pro Tree and the amateur Tree is one tenth of a second. It takes 0.500 seconds from the last amber to green on the amateur Tree and 0.400 from all the ambers to the green on the Pro Tree.

A common misconception is that as the green light lights, the timing starts, but in reality, the clock doesn't begin until you

> "The rollout distance (there is always some rollout) depends on what beam trips the clock. At some tracks it will be the Start ET Light, and at some tracks it will be as the Stage Light is unblocked."

From right to left: The pre-stage beam; the stage beam; and when used, the Start ET light. Some tracks use the Start ET light, while others have their clocks set to go when the stage light is unblocked.

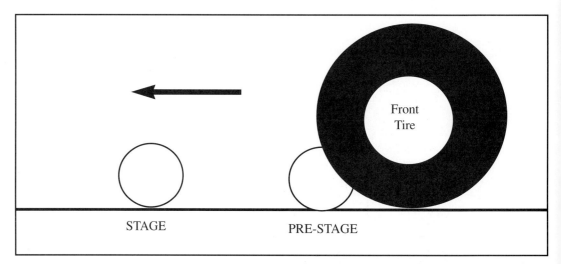

Stage carefully. The purpose of the pre-stage light is to let you know how close you are to the starting line. When it lights, creep forward until the stage light is lit. Illustration by Michael Lutfy.

move the car. The clocks begin timing as the car moves past the *rollout area*, the area between where the car is considered static and to where the clock begins. The rollout distance (there is always some rollout) depends on what beam trips the clock. At some tracks it will be the Start ET Light, and at some tracks it will be as the Stage Light is unblocked. Nevertheless, rollout is the distance the car is able to travel before the timers start.

What happens is that, first, the car rolls up to the starting line and as it moves forward,

it moves into a timing bean. The profile of the tire breaks the beam, which lights the pre-stage light on the Tree. As you move the car forward, the second beam is broken, setting off the stage light. At that point the cars are ready to start, and all that is left is the starter's push of the button which starts the Tree.

When the starter hits his button (don't bother trying to guess or time his movements—they are too crafty for that. Focus on the Tree), the sequence begins and the lights begin to flash. In other words, the

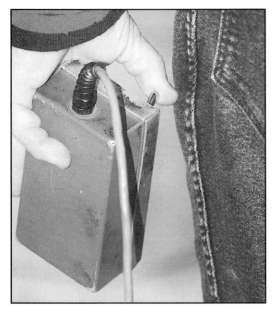

Starters are a crafty lot. They're trained to alter their routine, so trying to second guess them is a waste of time. Focus on the Tree, not in your rearview mirror.

Timing is done with an infrared light (left) beamed across each lane, reflecting off of foam timing blocks, at 60', 330', 660', 1000', 1254' (the first MPH clock) and 1320' intervals. When the car breaks the beam, time is recorded. The foam blocks are placed on the center line. Run one over and you'll incur the wrath of officials and fellow competitors if you cause a delay.

starter still manually sends the message to the Tree and the Tree does the rest. Once you either unblock the stage light, or break the Start ET beam, then your timed run begins. It is not when the light goes green.

Timing Clocks—At most tracks, each run is timed in increments. Some tracks at the bracket racing level will give you each intermediate time available, but not all of them will. On a typical professional dragstrip way, there may be timers located at the 60', 330', 660' (1/8 mile), 1000' and 1320'

Without reaction time factored in, there wouldn't be much point to racing two cars at the same time. One car could leave first, the other five minutes later and still both could hit their dial-ins. RT adds a human factor to the racing equation. Photo by Michael Lutfy.

the cells are aimed from the inside out, and for terminal speed and mid-track readings they are aimed at the center of the track. That's what those funny-looking foam blocks along the center line are for. They are moveable and very soft in case a driver loses control and hits one.

ELAPSED TIME

ET is the time it takes to go from the starting line to the finish line—period. But getting there first doesn't always mean you win.

REACTION TIME

As stated before, bracket racing is racing against your dial-in time. Whoever runs closest to that time wins the race. Since a bracket race is basically two cars that are racing against the clock, there needed to be a way that a winner could be decided by who actually ran a better race. If not, car A could leave first and run right on its dial-in and car B could sit at the line for five minutes. If car B exactly "nailed his index" also, who was the winner? Why even have a two-lane track if the cars are only racing the clock?! The thing that actually makes bracket racing a two-car sport is the reaction time. Another common way of expressing it is the word "light," as in the question "what kind of light did you cut on that run?" Reaction time is probably the single most important thing in all of bracket racing. Unfortunately for a beginner, it is a hard concept to understand fully.

Reaction time is literally defined as the amount of time elapsed between the green light coming on and the car actually breaking the start beam. Some timing systems are set up where a perfect reaction time is .000 seconds and others are set up with a perfect light being .500 seconds. The latter system is timed off the last yellow light coming on and since there is exactly .500 seconds

marks (see illustrations on pages 17 and 18). In addition, there are two mph timers, one 66' before the finish line, and one at the finish line. Your time slip may or may not give you all of these times and speeds.

All timing beams—from the stage and pre-stage to the mid-track timers and top end timers—work on a photoelectric basis with infrared beams. The light beams are mounted just above track level and are pointed at small reflectors. When the passing car trips the beam, it either starts or stops the clock, depending on where it's located. At the start,

HOW TO READ AN ET TIMESLIP

THE NHRA & WINSTON WELCOME YOU TO
INDIANAPOLIS RACEWAY PARK,
HOME OF THE 43RD U.S. NATIONALS

U.S. NATIONALS

	LEFT	RIGHT
Car#	202	121
Class	ST	ST
Dial	12.250	13.00
RT	.536	.510
60-ft	1.890	2.030
330-ft	5.29	5.60
1/8-mile	8.00	8.52
MPH	90.70	85.91
1000-ft	10.38	11.04
1/4-mile	12.38	13.08
MPH	112.40	106.28

This is a typical example of a timeslip from a "high visibility" dragway. You are supplied with the basic 60-foot time, quarter-mile ET and speed, as well as useful information via the 330-foot, 660-foot (eight mile), and 1000-ft ET and speed numbers. For the bracket race illustrated here, the winner is the one who gets there first, running closest to his dial-in. The participant in the left lane was quicker, but .13 seconds slower than his dial-in and had a slower reaction time than the person in the right lane. The right-lane racer ran closer to his dial-in, beating his opponent by .076-second—a package of RT and ET over the dial-in. Running quicker than dial-in, as you know, disqualifies the racer via a break out. If both cars break out, then the one with the bigger margin loses. Illustration courtesy *Hot Rod Magazine.*

between the last yellow and the green, a .500 reaction time would be perfect. Any way you slice it, it means the same thing: both cars left the line at exactly the same instant as the green light appeared. If the car leaves too soon by .010 seconds and red-lights, the reaction time would be .490 or -.010 depending on the system. Generally the .500 light system is most common so that's what we will use for our examples.

All this sounds neat and all but let's see how it affects our racing world. As mentioned above, one car could sit on the line for 5 minutes and still win the race by running right on the dial-in. This can't happen with this reaction time deal. The ET clock doesn't start timing until the car leaves the line. For example if you sit on the line with both the stage and pre-stage bulbs lit for 20 minutes before deciding to leave, you still can run a 10.97 ET. However the win light (race winner) is determined by a mathematical formula that involves a reaction time component as well as an ET component. These two components form what is called a "package." The timing computer compares the two racer's packages to a perfect package based on their dial-in and a perfect reaction time. Whoever came closer to this perfect package wins the race. This is why reaction time is so important. Let's do a few examples so illustrate this package concept.

Car A with 11.50 dial-in
Car B with 9.50 dial-in
.500 reaction time (RT) is perfect

Race 1
A runs 11.51 with .630 RT
B runs 9.60 with .515 RT

"If the faster car (who leaves second) already catches the slower car by half track, it's safe to assume that the slower car had a horrible reaction time. The key is to get your package as close to .000 as possible."

Who wins? On the surface it looks like car A wins because it ran much closer to the predicted dial-in. However car B gets the win light. Here's why:

Package A= .010 over dial-in + .130 over RT = .140 over pkg
Package B= .100 over DI + .015 over RT = .115 over pkg

Car B passed car A near the end of the track and got to the finish line first by .025 seconds. In this situation where A has a better ET run but still loses the race it is said that they "lost on a hole shot." The car did its job but the driver didn't! Generally it's not too fun to return to the pits after such a blunder.

Example 2. Same cars, same dial-ins:

Car A runs 11.82 with .505 RT
Car B runs 9.51 with .566 RT
Car A package .320 over DI + .005 over RT = .325 over pkg
Car B package .010 over DI + .066 over RT = .076 over pkg

Car B wins again. In this situation, it looks like car A's driver did the job by cutting a nice .505 light, but the car fell off somewhere and "couldn't run the number." This is why it's necessary to have a consistent car. Any variation to either ideal package and it's curtains.

Generally races will be much closer than these two examples. Most are decided by package differences of about .030 seconds. This will depend on where and when you are racing.

Having a good reaction time at the start allows for some breathing room for error down the track. It should be obvious as the race is going on who cut the better light. Ideally both cars should meet at the very end right at the finish line. If the faster car (who leaves second) already catches the slower car by half track, it's safe to assume that the

slower car had a horrible reaction time. The key is to get your package as close to .000 as possible.

Pro Reaction Timing—For professional classes like Top Fuel and Pro Stock the race is run "heads-up" or with no stagger to the Tree. These races are won in the old traditional way that whoever gets to the end first wins. Since one car could sit at the line for 20 minutes before leaving, the reaction time timer comes into play again to make sure both cars leave at the same time. In these pro classes, the Tree is set up to run what's called a "pro Tree." When this is going to happen, most Trees have a single blue light at the top that is illuminated to warn the driver that a pro Tree is coming. All three amber lights on each side flash on at the same time before the green flashes on. Usually the time interval between amber and green for the pro Tree is .400 seconds. Therefore a perfect light in pro Tree racing is a .400. However the package method is still used to determine the winner. Let's do a pro Tree, heads-up Pro Stock race example:

Car A: 7.045 ET, .467 RT Package = 7.045+.467=7.512
Car B 7.071 ET, .411 RT Package = 7.071+.411=7.482

Even though Car A had the faster run, it still loses to car B by .030 seconds. In pro Tree racing, the winner is decided by the fastest overall package. Most beginners will not encounter any pro Tree racing other than at the spectator level. However, all the new street legal shootout classes are run on the pro Tree, so if you plan on running in any of these, you will run on a pro Tree. ■

ELECTRONIC AIDS

6

Let's face it folks, we are living in a high-tech age. It seems that the computer chip is just about everywhere. Since a race car is also a piece of high-tech machinery, it was only a matter of time before the computer chip found its way into the bracket race car. Many people thought that once this hap-pened it was the "end" of real racing and that man had been replaced by a machine. Actually this is a very nearsighted thought, as nothing could be farther than the truth. Technology is always on the move and it can't be stopped. If you try to get in it's way, you will become the thing that is obsolete. I'm sure the people that complain about elec-

Like everything else these days, bracket racing has gone "hi-tech." There are quite a few electronic aids designed for the seri-ous bracket racer, from shift indicators to play-back tachs. Photo by Michael Lutfy.

"Actually, electronics in a modern bracket car are pretty simple and shouldn't be feared."

The transbrake button is usually located near the shifter. It essentially is a modified valve body that locks the transmission in reverse as well as first gear. Photo by Michael Lutfy.

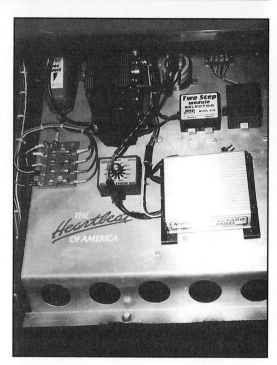

Installing electronics should be done neatly, such as this array above. Take the time to do a professional job. Photo by Michael Lutfy.

tronics in bracket cars also complained when the flat-head V8 was replaced by modern engines. Just like they got over that, they will eventually have to get over the modern electronics deal. And believe me, the human element has not been reduced. If anything the addition of electronics has actually increased the responsibility of the driver and crew.

STARTING LINE CONTROLS

Actually, electronics in a modern bracket car are pretty simple and shouldn't be feared. Basically there are two areas where electronics are used in a bracket car. The first area is to control and release the car on the starting line and the second area is to control (limit) the speed as the car goes down the track. Both devices are nothing more than glorified timers. Keep in mind that these devices are really only necessary for cars that run in the mid-12's and below.

Transbrake

As the speeds of even casual race cars

increased, it became pretty obvious that holding the car on the starting line with a high degree of consistency was becoming nearly impossible. With engines becoming more and more modified, a higher starting line rpm was needed. Holding the brake with your left foot and the gas with your right just wasn't going to hold back the 600 horsepower mill. A more solid way of preventing movement at the line was needed. This need gave rise to the "transbrake." This now-common device is nothing more than a specially modified automatic transmission valve body that locks the transmission in reverse as well as first gear. With this device energized, no power can be transferred through the transmission. When you decide to leave the line, you simply release the transbrake and the car instantly moves forward. You still must anticipate the green and release the trans-brake at the right time. So let's go through the procedure for using a transbrake.

Operation—Since the transbrake is only used on the starting line, all other preparations like the burnout are the same. You roll into the staging beams like normal and light the pre-stage light. This lets you know that you are about 6 inches away from the starting line. As the car creeps forward into the stage beam, you get ready to engage the transbrake switch. When the stage light comes on, you immediately press the switch in and hold it. At this point, the car will not roll any farther so you can take your foot off the "normal" brake. When you want to leave, simply release the button, floor the gas, and hang on. This works very well as you don't have to worry about the car creeping through the lights and red-lighting. However as with anything that works pretty well, racer's can make it work better. For example, since no power can go through the transmission with the transbrake on, you can floor the gas and the car still won't move. This will allow the engine to rev up right up to the torque converter's stall speed, which in a drag car can be as high as 5500 rpm.

Line Lock

A line lock consists of a cylinder that selectively modulates brake pressure in the brake lines, keeping them applied. In the past, racers only put them on the front wheels, so that the front brakes could be applied to hold the car while the rear wheels spun freely for the burnout. But the latest technology now requires you to put a line lock on all four wheels as well on just the front two. The solution is to install a split

If you're into long, smoky burnouts, a line lock will help keep the car still while the rear wheels spin. Photo by Michael Lutfy.

A line lock selectively modulates brake pressure in the brake lines. A typical installation is shown at left. At right is a common location for the button in a car without a delay box setup.

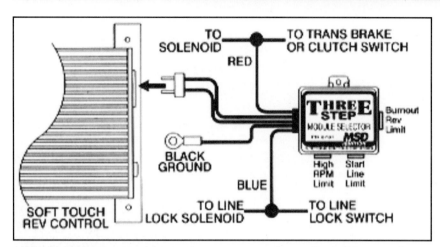

MSD's three-step system goes beyond the two-step by adding another rpm function specifically for burnouts. Of course, it also holds rpm consistent for staging, just like the two-step system. Illustration courtesy Autotronic Controls.

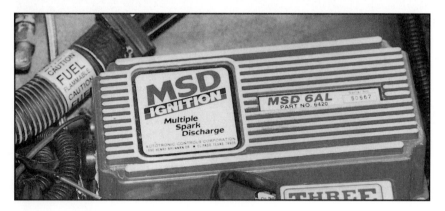

Adding bracket race electronics means you should upgrade your entire ignition system as well. Precise spark control is one more step in the quest for consistency.

Missed shifts, broken drivetrain parts and wheel spin can all send your engine way past redline, with catastrophic results. A rev limiter is recommended.

system, one which allows you to roll up and do your burnout while holding the front end and another which will allow you to hold the car at the line until it's time to go (unless you are using a transbrake, in which case you don't need to hold it for starting).

Two- or Three-Stepping

Now, with the engine screaming to 5500 rpm but the car not moving, when the brake is released the results are spectacular. Either the car leaves like a banshee or something in the drivetrain breaks! There had to be a more refined way to control the rpm while the transbrake was on. This method of control is called "two-stepping." Originally introduced by MSD ignition, the two-step ignition controller is simple yet effective. When using the MSD Two-Step Module Selector with one of MSD's Soft Touch Rev Controls, you can limit the rpm precisely while staged and waiting for the green light. By simply acti-

vating the transbrake switch, the Two Step module Selector will automatically switch to the lower rpm module and not allow the engine to rev beyond this point. When the starting light turns green and the transbrake switch is released, the car takes off and the Two Step will automatically switch back to the higher rpm limit. In this mode, the Soft Touch Rev Control will protect vital engine components against over-revving. This eliminates the starting line bog typical in most carbs. This method also allows the car to leave at precisely the same rpm each time, tremendously increasing the car's consistency, and improving your reaction times because you can precisely control engine rpm while the car is staged. Leaving the line is much easier since all that is now required is to stage, engage the transbrake, floor the gas and concentrate totally on the Tree. This transbrake and two-step deal works great, but because the cars are able to leave much harder with this system, red-lights are more common.

MSD's Three-Step Module Selector— With the addition of a new feature, MSD's Two Step Module Selector is available as a Three Step Module Selector. To increase the applications that this unit can be used in, a third rpm receptacle has been added. This third rpm function is designed for drag race applications and is to be activated when the car is in the water box during a burnout. By placing a preselected rpm module in the third receptacle, and activating it during the burnout, the engine will be protected against over-revving and allow for precise burnouts so that tire temperatures are kept consistent.

The Three-Step Module Selector can also be used to precisely hold the rpm consistent while staged and waiting for the green light, like the Two Step. Because the Three Step has to be used with a Soft Touch Rev Control or an MSD Ignition with built-in Rev Control, the final function of the Three Step is to protect the engine against missed shifts and over-revving.

Soft Touch Rev Control—The MSD Soft Touch Rev Control units protect an engine from over-revving, whether it is from a missed shift (common for most rookies), broken drivetrain or a loss of traction. Unlike many other types of rev limiters that simply cut off the ignition spark, the Soft Touch uses computer circuitry to drop one cylinder at a time and then fire that cylinder on the next cycle to prevent fuel from loading up the plugs. The result is very smooth rev limiting action that "holds" the engine at the selected rpm limit without backfires, extreme roughness or engine damage. The rpm limit is easily adjusted with plug-in modules.

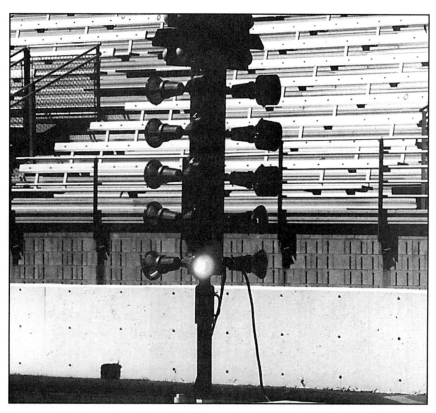

Red-lights are the bane of every drag racer's existence, but they are especially common for rookie racers. Cutting the light right is very difficult. Delay boxes can help you control your reaction time. Photo by Michael Lutfy.

Delay Box

Something must be done about this red-lighting problem. A solution came in the form of a delay box. This box is nothing more than a fancy timer that goes between the steering wheel button and the transbrake. Now when the button is released, the delay box timer delays the release of the trans-brake just enough to prevent a red-light. Since this amount of delay is adjustable, sharp racers figured out that they could change and therefore control their reaction times. They also figured that by simply adding more delay time into the delay box, they could actually leave when the first yellow light came on instead of trying to anticipate the last yellow going out. It is far easier to react to the first thing you see instead of trying to anticipate something. Typical delay time for an 11-second car is about .800 seconds. This will vary with how fast the driver, transmission, engine, and chassis

"In general, most drivers have found that on an amateur Tree you have a full second, give or take, before the time you can set for the car to go."

Dedenbear Products (510) 935-3025 has the U.S. patent on the theory of delay boxes. This model splices into the existing transbrake and/or roll-control circuits.

react. A faster car will need more delay since it moves away from the line faster. With this setup, you basically let go of the button and floor the gas at the same time and wait until the car leaves.

So you set the built-in delay off the top amber. The Tree is 1 1/2 seconds long and an average human being takes about 18/100s of a second to recognize the light come on and let go of the button. The cars will leave depending on how fast they are from 32 to 18-hundredths of a second at full throttle. So you let go of the button at the top amber and you have a second and a half.

A half a second of it is taken up in car movement and human reaction. The other second is what you have in the delay box which would hold the car until the last amber. As the Tree is turning green so too is your car moving out of the beam. It is much more consistent than guessing how close to the last amber you'll be.

In general, most drivers have found that on an amateur Tree you have give or take a full second before the time you can set for the car to go. In other words, taking into account the true reaction of seeing the first amber and moving accordingly, and the time it takes for the Tree to blink through two more ambers, added together with the time the car takes to get moving, approximately

one second will have passed for most drivers and cars.

Remember, you still have to change the number according to your situation and still have to hit the button, but you'll now be more consistent. If you'll eventually be running Super Pro—or Super Gas, Super Comp, Super Street Divisional Sportsman racing which also run a pro light—the amount of time between human reaction and the car running out of the beam is usually about 36/100ths. You may run 2 or 3 hundredths of a second delay since the delay boxes are adjustable to the 1,000ths.

Crossover Box—There is even a newer type of delay box called a crossover box that allows you to leave (release the button) when your opponent's first yellow comes on if you are the faster car. Remember that the slower car goes first so their light comes on first. This trick is handled by entering your dial-in and your opponent's dial-in into the crossover box. The computer simply takes the difference in the two dial-ins and adds it to your normal delay time setting. Again it's far easier to react to the absolute first thing you see, even if it's your opponents' Tree! You can delay up to 90 seconds in the box.

Delay boxes give you more control, not

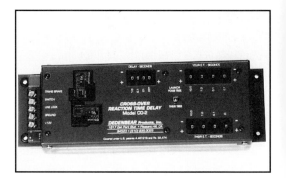

Dedenbear's crossover box has three sets of pushbutton switches. The quicker racer enters both dial-ins, along with the desired transbrake delay (if any). When he releases the transbrake button on his opponent's light, the unit calculates the handicap, adds the delay, and releases the transbrake at precisely the right time. Or, if the racer should draw a quicker opponent, a built-in toggle switch lets him cancel the crossover feature and use the unit as a standard delay box.

HOW TO SET DELAY BOXES
(Courtesy Dedenbear Products)

On an amateur or full Tree (.500, 3 amber tree), the best light to "leave" off is the top amber bulb. This is so the driver won't get "synchronized" to the Tree and accidentally anticipate the last amber or green light.

To leave off the top bulb, the driver should set the Delay box for 1.000 seconds. This should be close. Go out and make a trial pass. Collect your time slip and look at the RT. Whatever the time slip says for your RT, adjust the delay box the exact amount you wish to adjust the time slip!

If the time slip says you cut a .490 red light and you want a .505 light, adjust the delay box by that amount (.505 - .490 = .15). You want to add .015 to your time slip, then add .015 to your delay box. (1.000 + .015 = 1.015). Now, if everything stays the same (staging depth, driver's reaction, horsepower, traction, etc.), then you should cut a .505 light!

If the time slip says you cut a .550 light and you want a .505 light, adjust the delay box by the difference. (.505 - .550 = -.45). You want to subtract 0.45 from the delay box setting (1.000 - .45 = .955). You should now (theoretically) cut a .505 light. As you can see, the box doesn't guarantee a perfect light, it just becomes the driver's "adjustment knob." The driver must still let go of the button or hit the gas exactly the same every pass and stage the car exactly the same depth every run.

Crossover Delay—This means you are going to "crossover" and leave off of your opponent's top bulb, because he's much slower than you (ET-wise) and you don't want to be distracted by his Tree coming down, and his car launching and driving away. To simply crossover, you just add the difference in ET to your delay setting and let go of the button off his top his top bulb. If he's a 12.90 car and you're a 10.90 car, then the difference is exactly 2.00 seconds. Add this to your delay setting of 1.015 (as used in the above example), and you now have a total delay of 3.015 seconds.

As luck would have it, the ETs are seldom ever nice, even, round seconds. It's more like his car's dial is 12.86 and your dial is 10.42 seconds. so you have to be quicker than an accountant on April 14th to "do the math." The Dedenbear Crossover delay box has places to set your delay, your ET and his ET, so you leave the pits with 2 of the 3 settings already plugged in. When you know who you're paired up against, you just punch in his dial-in in the "Their ET" thumbwheel and the Dedenbear Crossover box will calculate the difference and add it to your delay setting.

more performance. At this point, that may bore you, but if you want to go anywhere in this sport, again, you'll need to be consistent. This is one modification to your car which will accomplish the result.

SPEED LIMITERS

The second area where electronics can come into play on your race car is controlling the car's acceleration as it motors down the track. Why would you want to slow the car down after you just spent thousands to make it faster? Simple. For example, if the car can run a 9.50 ET and we slow it down to an 11.50 ET, we have just gained a tremendous advantage over our opponent. This advantage comes into play as follows: Let's say we have two 11.50 cars on the line. My car can actually run 9.50 but I have

A speed limiter is handy if you're running a faster car that you've decided to run at a slower dial in, and will be running against a slower car. The limiter helps you gain a psychological advantage up on the top end.

Dedenbear's "Bear Stop" throttle stop controller is a plate style, mounted under the carb, and activated with either the pushbutton switch or an electronic timer. The switch attaches behind the shift lever so that the switch is "on" in low gear, and "off" in high gear. As long as the shifter is in low, you have WOT.

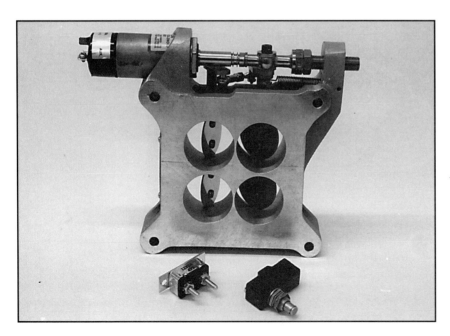

slowed it up to 11.50. Your car on the other hand can only run 11.50 flat-out. Since the dial-ins are both 11.50, both cars get to leave at the same time. Let's even say we both cut perfect .500 reaction times. As both cars are going down the track, my car kicks in an electronically controlled throttle stop that momentarily slows my car down. After a preset amount of time, the throttle stop opens back up and the engine starts to roar again. While this is happening, you immediately jump way out ahead of me and I have

to play catch up. This is no problem since I actually have the power to go 9.50. My advantage comes from the fact that I can watch (and therefore judge more accurately) your position the whole rest of the way down the track while you can't really see (or judge) me at all. All you will ultimately see is my car flying past you at the very, very end. This puts a lot less pressure on me and increases the chance that you will make a mistake at the end and lose the race. Since most bracket races are decided by less than .050 seconds, the room for error is extremely small.

Throttle Stop

Basically the electronic timer can slow the car down to a slower ET by actuating a throttle stop. This throttle stop is nothing more than a set of electronically controlled butterflies (just like in a carburetor) mounted in a plate just under the carb. When the throttle stop gets its signal from the timer, the butterflies close and slow the engine down.

Throttle stops are used either to slow a car to run a pre-determined ET (such as the "Super" classes) or to run a higher mph (miles per hour) for a given ET. Very often, the throttle stops are activated by a throttle stop controller.

The theory behind a controller is that since a car is moving very slowly at the start of a race, small changes in acceleration make large changes in ET; however, these changes make very little difference in the miles per hour at the end of the track. This is because the car is accelerating for most of the run under full power You can scrub off a lot of ET without really changing the mph. If you build a monster motor, you can run your original ET, but have a huge high speed charge at the top end. Running high mph means that you will be chasing your opponent down the track which is usually an advantage. You can watch both how fast you are overtaking your opponent and how quickly you are approaching the finish line, therefore making it easy to judge whether you should back off or not. Your opponent can't simultaneously see you and the finish line. He also can't judge how fast you are coming up on him, so you have the advantage.

Two or Four Stage—A two-stage controller allows you to leave the starting line at full throttle for minimum reaction time, shut off in the middle of the track to slow your ET, then come back on to give you a high mph finish. If your car is typically not the fastest, then one way to equalize the racing is to use a four stage controller. This allows you to turn on and off the stop again during the later part of a run so your opponent loses the advantage of being able to judge your speed and position at the finish line. A four-stage controller can be used as a 2, 3, or 4-stage controller, depending on how you program it.

Styles—All throttle stops can be operated by a throttle stop controller. There are two basic types of throttle stops, a "plate" style and a "linkage" style. The plate style bolts underneath the carburetor and contains its own set of butterflies that can be opened and closed by either an electric solenoid or a CO_2 actuator. An adjustable stop bolt sets the closed position of the blades. The "linkage" style stop is placed in the carburetor throttle linkage and limits how far the carburetor throttle can be opened. The linkage stop uses CO_2 for actuation. The "linkage style stop requires use of a throttle stop controller while the plate can be used with or without the controller.

Racing carburetors are designed to run in a wide open throttle condition. When they are run in a partially closed condition, the fuel metering doesn't maintain a constant air/fuel ratio as the air flow changes. The engine becomes sensitive to weather conditions and changes in the throttle stop settings don't produce predictable ET changes in the car. If a plate style throttle stop is used, the

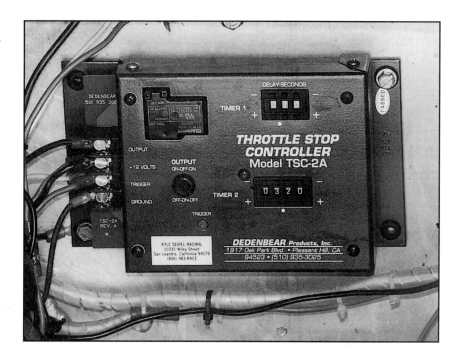

carburetor runs at wide open throttle at all times, and the total mixed air/fuel flow is regulated by the butterflies in the stop. The fuel metering stays constant. The weather has less effect on the engine, and changes in the stop settings become extremely predictable. This results in stable performance with rock-solid consistency. You can successfully run this stop in a closed condition for the entire length of the track if desired. A common setup is to mount a switch behind the shifter to have the stop close down when the car shifts. If you want a high mph run, this stop works equally well with a throttle stop controller.

The linkage-style stop is typically used when there is not enough hood clearance for a plate type stop or there are multiple carburetors or injectors. As discussed above, race carburetors are sensitive to partially closed throttle conditions. To minimize this problem, a throttle stop controller MUST be used with this type of stop. The trick here is to close the throttle almost all the way for the shortest amount of time possible at the immediate beginning of a run. By closing the throttle early and fully, maximum ET changes occur, so you keep the throttle

The Bear Stop can also be used with an electronic throttle stop controller. The controller replaces the shifter switch and the timer turns off and on the throttle stop as the car goes down the track.

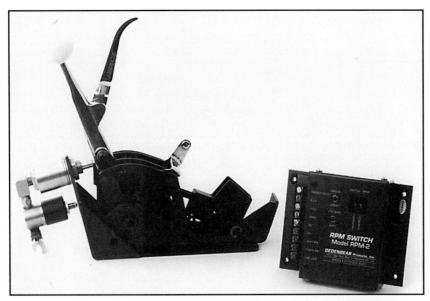

Rpm-controlled shifters are one of the most effective aids you can add. Many racers prefer the CO_2 style like this Dedenbear unit, because it is smaller and easier to tie in with a CO_2 throttle stop, if one is being used.

closed for the shortest possible time. This minimizes the amount of time that weather and other variables can affect the car. Successful cars using this type of stop are easy to spot at the track. They leap off the starting line and instantly die (sometimes it appears that they have broken), and then a second later explosively accelerate down the track. The violent reaction of the car creates one other problem: when the throttle goes to wide open again, the tires often break loose. To correct this problem, the Dedenbear CO_2 activated throttle stops have a needle valve adjustment (an industry first) that limits how fast the throttle opens back up. This allows you to tame the car down until it is consistent.

A linkage style stop can also be used as a staging rev limiter replacing an ignition 2-step box. Instead of holding the engine at a set rpm on the starting line by causing the ignition to break up, that linkage stop can be used to set the rpm by limiting how far the carburetor is open. You floorboard the gas pedal but the stop is set so that the engine will only run at the desired rpm. When you leave the starting line, the throttle goes to wide open. This is much easier on the engine

since you don't have ignition misfiring, flexing the crankshaft and having raw unburned gasoline washing oil off the cylinder walls.

Not For Beginners—The throttle stop can be an effective tool, especially in heads-up classes like Super Gas and Super Comp, but they are only as good as the person programming them. If the stop comes on for too long, the car will run too slow. The converse also holds true. Weather and track changes will also affect the car the same way. The best throttle stop users are the ones who are very familiar with their cars and document every run on paper to get an accurate feel for setting the throttle stops. At the local bracket race level, few if any racers use throttle stops. As a beginning racer, don't even think of getting involved with a throttle stop. Keep it as something to grow into as your experience increases.

Solenoid Shifters

One of the most effective products you can use to improve the consistency of your car is an rpm-controlled shifter. Shifts are made at exactly the same point in every run, which eliminates one of the major variables affecting the ET of the car. While rpm-controlled shifting improves all cars, two types of cars respond particularly well: heavy cars with low/medium power and light cars with high power. Low/medium horsepower engines need the transmissions' gear multiplication to accelerate heavy cars. Shifting to high gear removes the multiplication, greatly affecting the engine's ability to move the car. High-powered engines usually have a peaky torque curve and run through low gear quickly when installed in light cars. Shifting early or late ends up with the engine being far away from the desired torque range at the shift point. In both cases, it's easy to see that a slight change in the shift rpm makes a big change in the car's acceleration rate which causes an even bigger change in the ET.

Safety plays a role also, particularly with

high horsepower cars. An rpm-controlled shifter allows the driver to grab the steering wheel with both hands and concentrate on keeping the car straight during a run. A straight run is safer and more consistent.

Types of Shifters—Two types of rpm-controlled shifters are available, CO_2 or electric. Both work equally well and are a matter of driver preference. The shifters are controlled by an RPM2 switch module. This switch module determines the engine rpm by reading the pulses given off by the ignition system. These are the same pulses that are used by the tachometer. When the engine reaches the rpm that has been set in the rpm switch, the shifter is given a signal to shift the car.

Electric solenoid shifters are popular because they are simple and 12-volts are always available. These shifters mount behind your existing transmission shifter. They are automatically "cocked" when you pull the car into gear. At a predetermined rpm, a spring forces a ram to hit the shift lever and shift the car. These units draw very little power and are the utmost in reliability. Being simple, their only drawback is that they tend to be slightly longer and bulkier than CO_2 shifters.

Many racers prefer the CO_2 shifters because they tend to be smaller and more compact. Many times, the racer is also using a CO_2 throttle stop, so it is easier to tie in a shifter of the same type.

Making It All Work

To put this all back together: You come to the bleach or water box, bump on the foot brake and engage the line lock, do your burnout (figuring you have posi-traction or limited slip diff, at any rate). You move the car to the pre-stage lights, trip the stage lights, hit the transbrake button and now the car is static. You move off the brake and wait for the first light on the Tree. When the first amber light comes, you leave if you're using a crossover, or rev the throttle. The engine

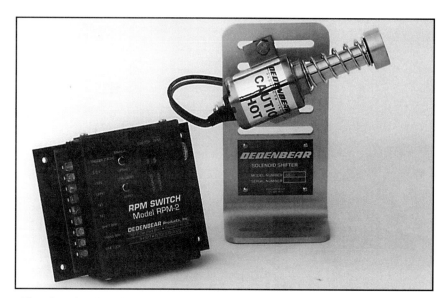

Electric solenoid shifters are a bit bulkier, but they are simple and easy to operate. Mounted behind your existing transmission shifter, they are automatically cocked when you pull the car into gear.

sputters and the car remains at the light. At the designated time set by the delay box, the ignition takes off full song, and away you go. If you're using one, the throttle stop kicks in mid-track or wherever you programmed it as well. It will stutter and stammer and then light a fire down the strip. You win. Hopefully.

After having said all of this, we must give you a word of caution: Most racers say that you should not be installing electronic aids until you've mastered leaving on your own. You'll never learn to be consistent until you've spent a season cutting lights manually.

GAUGES

If you're going to bracket race seriously and consistently, then you'll need to monitor what is going on with your car at all times. As you probably already know, street cars are seriously lacking when it comes to gauges. Most still function with an "idiot light" that illuminates when the problem has already occurred, and the damage done. If you're running a street car, like many bracket racers do, auxilliary gauges are highly

"You should be monitoring the oil pressure of your car constantly, keeping an eye out for any drop in pressure—shutdown the engine immediately if you do."

Nice, clean, easily readable, purpose-built dash. You'll need oil, water, and volt gauges at the very least. Photo by Michael Lutfy.

recommended. Two of the biggest players are Auto Meter and VDO.

Recommended Gauges

You need at least an oil pressure gauge, a volt gauge, a water temp gauge, and a tachometer. You should be monitoring the oil pressure of your car constantly, keeping

Gauges provide valuable feedback about what your car is doing, and the standard idiot lights don't give you enough information. If there's no room inside or you don't want to chop up your dash, a hood mounted set is an option.

an eye out for any drop in pressure—shutdown the engine immediately if you do. That way you don't have to wait for the idiot light to know there's a terminal engine problem which, by the time you finally get the info from the light, is already too late. Same thing with water temp. If the needle is pegged to the right, you better think about what you're going to do for a ride home. Perhaps it is nothing more than a stuck thermostat, but you better do something about it now, not wait until the coolant overflow explodes and you've got all the Safety Safari guys giving you dirty looks because you spread coolant all over the starting line.

The tach is a must for several reasons. First, it keeps you from redlining and floating a valve, or breaking a valve spring, rocker arm or whatever. A factory manual should be able to tell you the rpm where peak torque and peak horsepower occur (the powerband). This knowledge is important for launching and shifting, and for gearing. A tach can help you gauge your performance and speed. As you jam through the lights at the far end note your rpm. If you are not at the peak horsepower rpm by the time

you reach the end of the track, you need to adjust your gear ratios to get the powerband up quicker. An oversize tach is sometimes mounted on the hood, in plain view.

As you advance and develop your skills, you may consider looking at such advanced gauges as shift lights, and Tach Playback Recorders.

Auto Meter

Auto Meter has been one of the leading developers of drag racing instruments since the beginning of the sport. More often than not, the aftermarket gauges on a drag racer have the Auto Meter label. Here's a sampling of their latest technology.

Gauges—Auto Meter's performance gauges are designed for the Sportsman

through Pro classes. All Sport-Comp mechanical and electric gauges are quality engineered to meet the highest racing standards.

Auto Meter's Pro-Comp mechanical gauges are liquid-filled to help dampen vibrations in the most severe race applications. The gauge mechanism is sealed in the case and filled with a special vibration dampening liquid. The liquid helps to absorb vibration and stabilize needle movement while maintaining accurate readings. The dampening effect allows the gauge to remain in top functioning condition and prolongs gauge life. These 2 5/8" liquid-filled gauges are available in: fuel pressure, oil pressure, oil temperature, water tempera-

Auto Meter's Pro Comp gauges are liquid-filled to help dampen racing vibrations. Courtesy Auto Meter.

Auto Meter's Ultra Lite gauges are made of lightweight anodized aluminum. Courtesy Auto Meter.

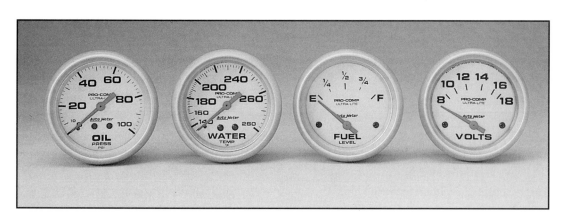

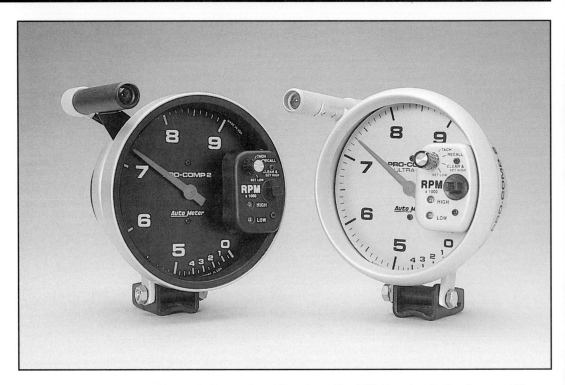

Shift-Lite tachs offer the ability to dial-in precise shift points. The Shift-Lite signals the time to shift, and the dual purpose "set" button is held during dial-in to guard against accidental changes and can then be pressed to recall the shift-point for instant verification.

ture, blower pressure, vacuum, brake pressure and transmission temperature.

The hottest gauges for sportsman and professional racers in any motorsports are the Ultra-Lite gauges. Auto Meter's Ultra-Lite gauges weigh about half the weight of the Sport-Comp gauges without sacrificing any quality. The anodized aluminum dial with florescent red pointers make the Ultra-Lite gauges extremely easy to read even in dark interiors.

Tachs—Auto Meter offers many tachometers that are designed for high performance race applications. Models are available with rpm ranges of 8,000, 9,000, 10,000 and 11,000 with or without shift lights. Models with the high rpm recall option will show the highest rpm during an entire race.

The Shift-Lite tachometer is another innovation in instrument technology from Auto Meter. This new Shift-Lite tach features "dial-in exactness." While you are dialing-in your desired shift point, the tachometer

pointer moves, indicating the rpm being selected. Under normal operation, the Shift-Lite signals when the engine reaches the exact rpm that the pointer registered during dial-in. The dual purpose "set" button is held during dial-in to guard against accidental changes and can then be pressed to recall the shift-point for instant verification. The shift-point can be easily changed—even in staging just prior to a race. The high intensity amber Shift-Lite, mounted directly on the tach, is bright enough for daylight racing and is ideal for the critical no-look shifting demanded in drag racing.

Auto Meter's Playback Series—If you really want to step up, consider Auto Meter's Playback technology. Auto Meter has really developed their series of Playback tachs and peripherals to help you get as much data as possible about your run, without having an onboard computer.

Auto Meter's Sport-Comp Playback Tach will record and play back your entire run with the ability to stop the play back at any

Here's a trick setup: Auto Meter's Ultimate Playback Tach. With this setup, you can record and play back your entire run with the ability to stop the playback at any point. Recordings begin at the actual launch which allows you to play back your race from the beginning.

point. Recordings begin at the actual launch which allows you to play back your race from the beginning. Recorded data is sampled at a rate of 30 bits per second for a smoother, more accurate recording. These recordings show engine rpm through your entire run. All shift points are recalled, with any slippage in your transmission or clutch being clearly shown during playback. This information is beneficial when fine tuning your chassis and selecting different gear ratios and tire sizes.

The Pro-Tech Printer Interface directly downloads a Playback Tach, Playback Recorder, or LTM to a printer without the need for a computer. The output from the printer shows a comparison of rpm to time, enabling the racer to see important high and low rpm, and shift points during a race. By looking at the printed run, you can check the

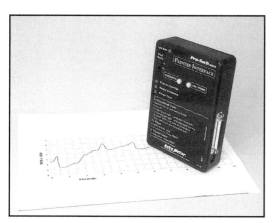

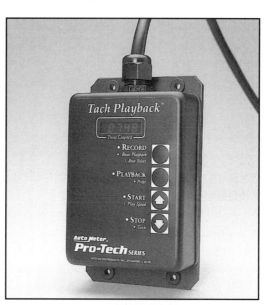

The printer interface allows you to "dump" the information recorded by the tach without a computer. The Playback box allows you to convert any Auto Meter tach to Playback. With this system, you can fine tune your chassis and engine for consistency. You'll be able to compare different tracks against different combinations in gearing, chassis and engine setups.

"All shift points are recalled, with any slippage in your transmission or clutch being clearly shown during playback. This information is beneficial when fine-tuning your chassis and selecting different gear ratios and tire sizes."

The Top Eliminator DSP (dual shift-point), is one of the industry's most accurate and cost-effective microprocessor-based tachometers. It is designed with two memories: a 200-second memory with a sample rate updated 5 (times per sec), and a 50-second memory with sample rate-updated 20 times per second.

setup. The launch rpm is seen along with the amount of drop when the throttle stop is activated. As the rpm's rise, you can see the point of converter lock up and see exactly when the shift occurred. This real-time data allow you to double check the auto settings after each run. Runs printed can now be used to compare different tracks or different combinations in chassis, gearing, tires and engines. This information can prove to be a very important tool when tuning your car for optimum performance and consistency.

If you already have a good Auto Meter tach, you can convert it to playback with Auto Meter's new Tach Playback Recorder. Full quarter- or eighth-mile runs can be recorded and played back at full or half speed. The time that is spent in each gear is also displayed on an LED clock running at full or half speed. Four separate runs at up to 40 seconds each can be recorded in high

capacity memory. The recordings are started by the release of the line-lock or trans-brake with Auto Meter's exclusive ARMS (Automatic Record Memory Start). After the run the Playback will display the entire race from start to finish on your tachometer. The printer interface described above is also available to allow you to download the recordings directly to a printer without the need for a computer.

VDO

VDO North America has just expanded its Pro Cockpit White Series Instrument line with the addition of two new VDO Eliminator Tachometers. They include the Top Eliminator DSP and Comp Eliminator II, each offered in 9,000 and 11,000 rpm models. The Top Eliminator DSP features VDO's innovative Dual Shift Point (DSP) Technology, which allows it to be programmed for two separate shift settings.

Gauges—VDO's Pro Cockpit White Series is the result of years of competition experience and strict design and test procedures. The highly legible, quick reading, 2-5/8" dia. dials have helped make them a favorite among top racing teams as well as in other motorsports circuits. They are extremely lightweight and feature 360° internal balanced lighting.

The Pro Cockpit White line includes both mechanical and electrical instruments. The mechanical versions feature precision machined movements and are offered in Water Temperature, Pressure and Turbocharger instruments. Electrical instruments include Fuel Level and Voltmeter.

DSP—VDO's innovative Dual Shift Point (DSP) Technology, as used on the Top Eliminator DSP, is one of the industry's most accurate and cost-effective microprocessor-based tachometers. It is designed with two memories: a 200-second memory with a sample rate updated 5x per sec. And, a 50-second memory with sample rate updated 20x per sec. All replays are shown at 1/3 speed. During memory replays, the built-in LED functions as a clock, displaying the actual elapsed time recorded.

The Pro Eliminator DSP is ideal for applications requiring only peak rpm recall. Maximum RPM is recorded electronically and then digitally displayed on the tach's bright LED readout. The LED display allows settings of shift points in increments of 10 RPM. Set points can be reset as required.

Shift Lights—Both new Eliminator tachometers work with VDO's Mega-Lite Shift Light. This bright 8-LED shift light responds instantly and is controlled by the Eliminator Tach to within an accuracy of 2 RPM. Both tach and shift light can be mounted on dash, steering column or roll bar.

Tachs—VDO Eliminator tachometers are designed to work with 4, 6 and 8 cylinder

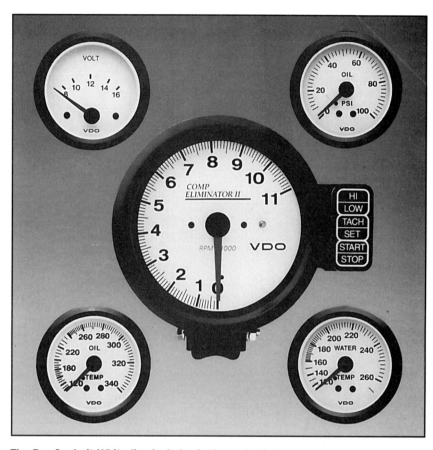

The Pro Cockpit White line includes both mechanical and electrical instruments. The mechanical versions feature precision machined movements and are offered in Water Temperature, Pressure and Turbocharger instruments. Electrical instruments include Fuel Level and Voltmeter.

engines and are compatible with 12 V standard and electronic ignitions such as MSD, Mallory, Accel and Allison. An optional Vertex Magneto adapter is available. The remote Touch Control Pad can be mounted up to 6 ft. from the tach with an optional kit. VDO's Eliminator Tachometer Series is the result of years of competition experience and stringent design and test procedures. Their ruggedness, reliability and exceptional performance have helped make them a favorite among top professionals and weekend racers. ∎

ENGINE & SUSPENSION TIPS 7

Do you need a tricked-out motor with nitrous to enjoy bracket racing? Not at all—but it sure is fun! Remember, it's more important to run consistently than it is to run fast. Photo by Michael Lutfy.

The intention of this book has been to get you started on the sport of bracket racing. Once hooked, the amount of money you can spend on building a super 8-second bracket car is just about limitless. You can go all out, with a tube-frame chassis, aluminum body panels, blown, injected big-block, etc. But until that time comes, you are probably going to stick with more modest equipment. This book is not a how-to technical manual to help you build an engine, or to help it go faster. However, there are some very basic tuning and maintenance procedures, as well as some easily performed modifications, that can help you get the most from your bracket racer, regardless of make or model, and budget. It can also help make your

If you have a choice, a big block is preferred. It is stout and can produce more power more consistently than a comparable small block. This setup amounts to serious overkill for the casual weekender. Photo by Michael Lutfy

weekend go a bit smoother. When it comes to suspension and chassis preparation, again, our aim is to give you some basics to help you prepare the most consistent bracket racer possible. To that end, the sections on "Tuning Leaf Springs," and "The Front Suspension" have been reprinted with the permission of *Hot Rod* magazine.

ENGINES

Every racer knows that the engine is the heart of the race car. It is certainly the easiest thing to modify to prepare to race. Most racers are content to beef up the internals, dress it up with chrome goodies and let it rip down the track. If the car doesn't go fast enough, whip out the VISA and buy more parts for the engine. However bracket racing isn't really a race of speed. The 13-second car can just as easily be a winner as the 8-second car. Consistency is the goal here. Many racers don't know that consistency can actually be built into an engine during its rebuild. Previous chapters have drilled into

you that in order to win, you must do everything exactly the same each and every time. This is also true of the engine. Everything must work exactly the same on every run. This means no leaky or worn rings, gaskets or valves. This also means regular maintenance by the owner.

Engine Choices

Engine choice will usually be determined by the owner's preference in vehicles. Cross breeding a different brand engine into your car is not a good plan especially for a beginner. Stick with something that can be installed easily. Believe me, there will be more than enough other problems to deal with. Generally for a beginner, a big-block engine is the preferred setup for a drag car. Even in stock form they will produce more power than a mildly modified small block and they will be more consistent to boot.

Most big-block engines were originally designed to move around big heavy cars for 100,000+ miles. As a result they are very stout pieces. This is ideal for a drag engine.

> *"Generally for a beginner, a big-block engine is the preferred setup for a drag car. Even in stock form they will produce more power than a mildly modified small block and they will be more consistent to boot."*

If you're having an engine rebuilt, perhaps the single most important thing you can do is to make sure that the machine shop uses a torque plate when machining the cylinder bores. **Photo by Michael Lutfy**

These heavy-duty castings make for an engine that will stay sealed even under high loads. Since more power is available due to the large displacement, the rpm level can be kept down which will increase durability as well. A large displacement, low rpm engine will last a lot longer than a smaller, more highly stressed small block.

Building a Consistent Engine

Again, it is way beyond the scope of this book to get into the details behind building an engine. If you're interested in this, there are many HP auto books available (see listing on the last page of this book) that will help you build your own. But if you are building an engine yourself, or having one rebuilt, there are certain things you should do that will help increase the consistency of the engine. By consistency, we mean the performance output.

Machining—When the engine is being rebuilt, make sure that the machine shop uses a deck plate when honing the cylinders. This deck plate is torqued on the block while the engine is being honed to simulate the stress and distortion caused by the cylinder head bolts. With the plate on, the cylinders will be straight and round when the heads are installed. This will give the best ring seal possible since the rings can only seal well on a round surface.

On the subject of ring seal, try to swing the few extra bucks on file to fit rings. These rings will allow the engine builder to fit each ring gap to each cylinder. This will keep blow-by to a minimum, extending engine life in the process. Some racers are actually so concerned about cylinder wall flex and distortion during operation that they fill some of the waterjackets of the block up with cement! This is done to keep the cylinder walls as rigid as possible to allow the ring seal to remain perfect. This filling of the block is fine for a drag car but is definitely a no-no for a street/strip car like at typical bracket racer.

Always mill the deck surfaces of the block and heads to ensure the gaskets will seal well.

Lightweight Components—Lightweight pistons and rods are also a good choice since the lighter parts will stress the engine less and they will also allow the engine to rev quicker. These lightweight components are about the only things that will make the car go faster and at the same time keep the engine together longer.

Cylinder Heads—Make sure the valve guides in the heads are also tight. These guides control the valve as it moves in the head. If the guides are worn, the valve won't hit the seat in the same spot each time and leakage will occur. If this happens, both power and consistency will be lost. It is a good idea to have the stock cast iron guides replaced with the longer wearing bronze variety. Check to be sure that the valve springs have enough load and clearance to work with the cam that was chosen. If the springs are too weak, the valves will float at high rpm and again power and consistency are thrown out the window.

When assembling a new purpose-built race engine, make sure you use lightweight aluminum pistons and rods. The reduced rotating mass of the bottom end allows the engine to rev quicker.

Balancing the crank and rods won't really make consistency, but it will free up power resulting in a faster ET slip. If a piston change was done, the crank must be rebalanced.

Basically it all boils down to having a big, low rpm engine that was machined and assembled accurately. If all of these things are done correctly, the engine should reward you with many hundreds of consistent passes and hopefully a few winner checks.

Engine Tuning Tips

Generally an engine will run more consistently if the fuel mixture is slightly on the rich side. This will also help prevent detonation in the long run by preventing any lean out condition that may occur. If the car is jetted too rich, however, it may become lazy and unresponsive. I would recommend starting with the stock jet sizes for your particular carb and increase (richen) the jet sizes one step at a time and watch the mph of the run. Always tune for mph, not ET. If the mph goes up, continue to richen until no further increase is noticed. At this point, go one size richer than the jet size of maximum

mph and you should be set. Obviously if the mph falls when the carb is richened, then start leaning the jets until the point of maximum mph. Of course this requires a lot of patience, but the information will be very valuable. Also, don't run the timing too far advanced, as this can promote engine-destroying detonation, especially if you get a load of bad gasoline. Check your timing at the point where the car is shifted. If it appears unsteady, try tack welding the advance weights in the distributor. This will eliminate all the advance in the distributor so starting may be a little harder, especially when the engine is warm. This locked distributor should make the timing mark appear much steadier at high rpm. This means that the spark is occurring at exactly the same time each and every time. This is what is required of every system in the race car (including the driver) to make the car a winner at bracket racing.

SUSPENSION

Keeping in mind the fact that all you're doing on a dragstrip is going straight—or at work most efficiently. Without a well-designed chassis and suspension, all the power in the world doesn't mean diddly and the car will never realize its potential. It'll do a great burnout, yeah, but it'll also do a great burnout when you'd rather be three car lengths ahead of the other guy. Without a properly prepared suspension system, all that expensive grunt is wasted. Leaf springs can be made to work very well for drag racing. We do have a few ways to tune them up though. The good news is that you can coerce those simple leaf springs of yours into doing the same job as a four-link and coilovers to stick the tires to the tarmac.

Weight Transfer & Suspension Dynamics

You're certainly familiar with the term "weight transfer." When the car launches, the front wheels come up, sometimes off the ground, and that puts more weight on the rear tires, which helps them get traction. If both front wheels are off the ground, 100 percent of the vehicle's weight is on the rear tires, so theoretically they should have maximum traction. That's a gross oversimplification of what is really happening, but it helps explain how the tires are "planted" with body movement. Weight transfer doesn't just occur front-to-back. The rotation of the engine also comes into play. Imagine looking at the rear of the car. Remember that the crankshaft turns counterclockwise (viewed from the flywheel), which makes the engine block rotate in the opposite direction (action reaction) and lift the driver side of the frame (that's why motor mounts always break on the driver side). The energy from the crank is ultimately relayed to the third member, where another set of reactive forces applies. As power is applied to the rearend, the front of the rearend housing rotates upward. Because the tires are stuck to the ground, the pinion gear tries to climb the ring gear instead of turning the tires, which causes the axle housing to rotate. The

Nitrous oxide is no laughing matter. Make sure your driving skills, and your car, are up to handling the extra power, and that you have sufficient mechanical skills to fine-tune the air/fuel mixture to compensate for the nitrous. If it gets out of balance, you'll fry the motor before mid-track. Photo by Michael Lutfy.

the most, perhaps making a slight left or right turn from the staging lanes up to the line—you might wonder just why the suspension is important at all. But like everything else in drag racing, consistency is the sum of all little things. This is a sport of very slight tolerances, where no one thing is critical, but where every little bit adds up.

TUNING LEAF SPRINGS

There is the matter of power, and then there is the matter of putting that power to

When you launch, the weight from the front of the car is transferred rearward, putting more of the vehicle's weight on the rear tires, helping them with traction. In theory, if both wheels are up, then 100% of the weight must be on the rear tires—but there are other factors as well.

housing also rotates side to side in reaction to torque. The right-side tire at the back of the car lifts toward the body and the left-side tire gets pushed away from the body. When you combine these motions with the front-to-rear weight transfer and watch the car leave, it looks like the body is putting a lot of weight on the right rear tire. In fact, the torque is trying to pull that right rear off the ground, and plant the left rear. That's why the right rear tire is usually the one that spins.

Is the Car Tracking Straight?

Watch fast cars leave the line and you'll notice that every one of them reacts differently. Sometimes the car turns to one side, forcing the driver to correct with the steering wheel. A car that pulls is not planting both tires effectively, and therefore not getting proper bite. It's also dangerous. Before adding a traction device to the car, the chassis must be inspected for things that keep the car from going straight. Is the housing mounted straight in the chassis? Bent or twisted housings, worn-out bushings, bent leaf springs, or unevenly adjusted ladder bars will cock the rearend in the car. Where the rearend housing goes, the car goes, and this must be perfectly straight ahead. Even if the rearend is plumbed straight, a flexing chassis, suspension parts and axle housing, or a combination of ineffectual shock-mount location, worn-out springs, incorrect or uneven preload, and uneven tire pressure are all liable to steer the car off course. Furthermore, an undercarriage that hasn't been strengthened to resist torsional forces with subframe connectors or a rollcage will

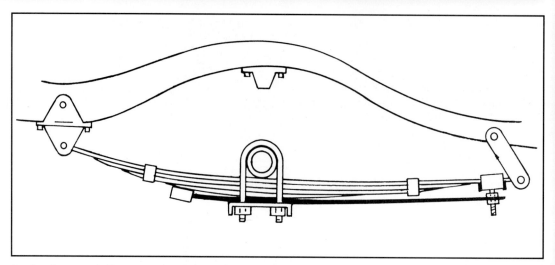

Leaf springs are bulky and heavy, but they represent a simple and effective way to locate and suspend the rearend. Unfortunately, they tend to bend under hard acceleration.

"Finally, the obvious: An uneven water burnout heats up one tire more than the other and makes it stickier. If the left rear tire hooks better than the right rear, the car will turn right."

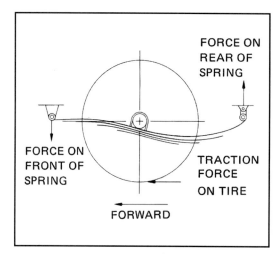

This shows what happens to a leaf spring during hard acceleration. The torque reaction on the axle twists the spring into the S-shape above.

be impossible to tune successfully.

All this twisting and rotating is abusive, especially to an unmodified axle housing. Spring perches and axle tubes twist a bit under high-torque loading, and that plays hell with the rear suspension, too. In a drag race car or serious street machine, the spring perches must be gusseted and the factory welds inspected for full coverage. Things such as worn or broken springs and uneven tire pressure seem simple enough to check, but you'd be surprised at the number of racers who don't bother. Finally, the obvious: An uneven water burnout heats up one tire

more than the other and makes it stickier. If the left rear tire hooks better than the right rear, the car will turn right. All the above variables should be duly noted or fixed outright before you install a traction device.

The Nature of the Leaf Spring

Leaf springs are bulky and heavy, but they represent a simple and effective way to locate and suspend the rearend. Unfortunately, they tend to bend under big power. As power is applied to the rearend, the front of the housing rotates upward. The rearend is bolted to the leaf springs, and when the housing rotates it bends the leaf front into an S shape and pulls the tire off the ground. The spring snaps back violently, but power is still being applied so it happens over and over again, causing the tires to bounce up and down with a vengeance. This is called "wheelhop." The primary purpose of a rudimentary traction device is to keep the spring from wrapping up and to keep the tires on the ground, although some devices serve other purposes as well.

Think of a leaf spring as two separate entities. The spring's front half locates the housing in the chassis; the rear half is responsible for most of the "spring" function. The front half wraps up under power, pulling the tire

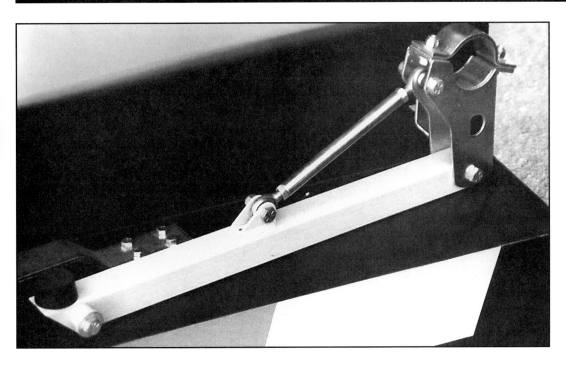

The Lakewood traction bar bolts to the axle tubes and the lower trailing arm bolt. Installing a set will provide a significant improvement for the stock suspension.

off the ground. The stiffer the spring's front half is, the more resistant it is to wrapping up. That's one of the keys to the success of the legendary Chrysler Super Stock leaf springs. The front half is shorter and stiffer than "normal," and designed to preclude the use of any type of traction device whatsoever. A leaf spring custom-made from thicker steel and with increased spring rate has more natural resistance to bending. John Calvert successfully runs a four-speed '68 Cobra-Jet Mustang in NHRA Super Stock on 9-inch tires and competes against wheel-tubbed cars that are usually equipped with automatic transmissions. The combination of the four-speed and little tires is a challenge to hook up, but he does, using leaf springs with a lot of rate and a low arch. The high rate helps keep the springs from bending and the body level on launch, and the low arch is necessary to keep the ride height as low as possible. However, the spring rate he prefers makes the car so stiff it'll knock your fillings out over pebbles in the road.

Types of Leaf Springs—There are two types of leaf springs: multileaf (which usually have between three and five leaves, each one progressively shorter than the next), and the monoleaf type (with a single

main leaf). The monoleaf is light and locates the rearend, but it wraps up much easier and usually requires a traction device to work.

Traction Aids

The leaf spring benefits from a wide variety of traction aids to make the car launch like a Super Stocker, and most are easy bolt-ons that don't require a ton of tuning. We'll take a look at the most common devices and explain how they work and how to tune them.

Spring Clamps—Spring clamps are so simple to make, you can do it in the privacy of your home. Clamping the leaves together on the front half of the spring is one way to solidify it and make it more resistant to wrap-up. The clamps force the rear half of the spring to work harder, so it'll wear out faster, and longer spring shackles are usually required to maintain the ride height and allow that part of the spring sufficient movement.

Traction Bars—These are known as traction bars, but "slapper" is more accurate because they actually slap up against the bottom of the leaf spring. The slapper bar bolts solidly to the leaf spring and to the rearend housing at the mounting pad. In fact,

"The Cal-Tracs system allows slight changes to the instant center (or "pushing point" of the rear suspension, and it also prevents leaf-spring wrap-up through methods different from anything else available)."

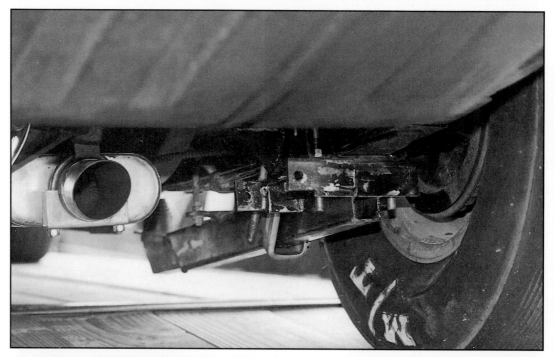

Traction bars are mounted directly to the rearend, on the axle housings, at the same level as the pinion gear. When the rear axle housing twists upward during hard acceleration, the rubber snubbers on the front of the bars contact the frame rails, which effectively redirects the torque to the rear and levers the axle downward, planting the rear tires on the ground. Traction is obviously enhanced, and you're out of the hole with plenty of grip.

most slapper bar designs replace the stock lower mounting pad. As the housing rotates, so does the bar, which contacts the front portion of the leaf spring and keeps the rearend from rotating further and the spring from becoming S-shaped. A rubber snubber is mounted between the slapper bar and the spring to soften initial contact. Slapper bars are very easy to install, they allow some pre-load to be dialed into the spring, and they're inexpensive—all of which makes them the world's most popular traction aid.

Southside Bars—The Southside bar bolts solidly to the bottom of the rearend housing spring mount, and clamps securely to the front of the leaf (depending on the applica-

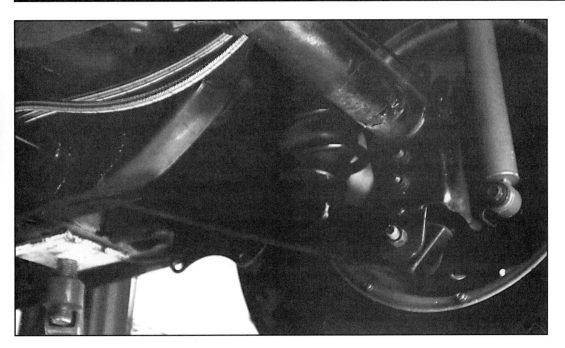

The popular Southside Machine Co. traction bars, shown here on a late-model Mustang, move the lower trailing arm pickup approximately 2-1/2" out from the stock location. Moving the pickup points alters the instantaneous center location, which creates a lifting action that plants the slicks firmly to the track for a much improved launch.

tion), just behind the mounting eye. It changes the lifting point of the suspension and, when the housing rotates, the bar pushes up on the body (hence "lift bar") and plants the tire.

Cal-Tracs Bars—Through his Super Stock experience, John Calvert has invented (and patented) the Cal-Tracs traction device, and many of his competitors are now running it on their cars. The Cal-Tracs system allows slight changes to the instant center (or "pushing point") of the rear suspension, and it also prevents leaf-spring wrap-up through methods different from anything else available). Calvert also claims that it helps handling in corners, so it can be used on dual-purpose vehicles.

Pinion Snubbers—A pinion snubber is similar to a slapper bar, but it applies force to the top of the rearend housing instead of the spring. The pinion snubber is a rubber bumper mounted to the floorpan (sometimes the pinion snout itself, e.g., Mopar applications), just above the pinion snout of the rearend housing. When the housing rotates, it contacts the snubber, which stops the rota-

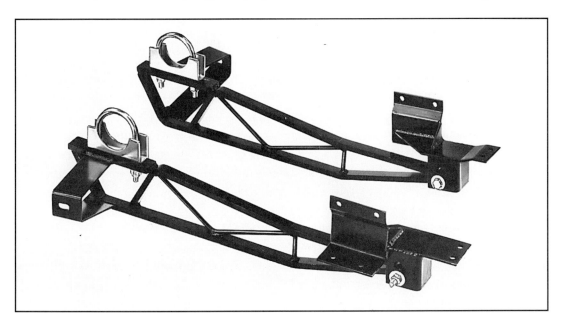

Hooking up the rear tires means controlling the axle windup. Competition Engineering's bolt-on ladder bars are quick and easy to install. These bars are lightweight and well engineered.

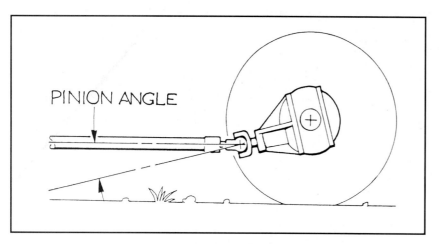

PINION ANGLE

Set the static pinion angle so that the pinion is pointing down in relation to the driveshaft. Leaf-spring cars without ladder bars usually need 5-7 degrees of pinion angle, compared to 2-3 degrees for ladder bars and 1-2 degrees for four-links. Courtesy *Hot Rod* magazine.

tion and helps prevent spring wrap-up. As with a slapper bar, many racers adjust the snubber so it touches the rearend (or floorpan) in a static mode; some use it to preload the pinion.

Ladder Bars—Ladder bars are normally used with coilover shocks, but they can be used with leaf springs that have a housing floater. The ideal length of a ladder bar is longer than the front half of the leaf spring, and one of its functions is to locate the rearend. If the ladder bar and leaf spring are both locating the rearend, and their lengths are different, the arcs they follow will also differ and eventually bind the suspension. Floaters allow the rearend housing to slide back and forth on the springs a small amount. The springs still support the vehicle, but the ladder bars locate the rearend and transfer the energy of movement from the housing to the chassis. The advantage to ladder bars is that they provide a longer lever to act on the car (compared to a leaf spring) and the ability to change the instant center and pinion angle, and therefore the "hit" on the tire. Ladder bars are more violent than bolt-on traction devices and four-links, and they're not much fun on the street, but they work very well on the dragstrip and allow more compensation for varied track conditions than slapper bars.

Preload

Sometimes, no matter how well the chassis is sorted out, the car still won't go straight. In this case, the suspension can be preloaded on one side. This means that the traction device exerts force on the spring while the car is sitting still. This is equivalent to additional rate to just one spring. Whichever way the car turns, the tire on that side isn't doing its job, so adding more rate to that side in the rear may straighten the car out. Many racers set up their cars with just a touch of preload on both sides. If the car only goes straight when the preload is different side to side, there's something wrong with either the car (weight distribution is off, the rearend isn't straight, the frame is bent, or the tires aren't of equal pressure or pliability) or the surface of the race track. Most traction devices can be adjusted for preload, some easier than others.

Pinion Angle

Pinion angle, defined as the angle of the pinion gear in relation to the drive shaft, is critical to the whole, but many racers don't know what it affects, or they simply ignore it. On a street car with street tires, pinion angle can be useful in getting the car to hook up. Ideally, as the car moves down the track under power, the pinion angle should be zero degrees. Because the rearend rotates (and the pinion rises) under power, when at rest, the pinion must be pointed down slightly so that it is at zero when under power. The less the static pinion angle (the closer to a straight line it is with the driveshaft), the harder the suspension hits the tires. On a slippery track or on the street, more pinion angle will shock the tires less and help them bite better.

Shock Absorbers

Leaf springs and traction devices, with their various mounting options, rates, and so forth, are adjusted to get the suspension close to optimum, but shock absorbers are

These Air Lift air bags will improve traction when installed on rear coil springs. Shown here is a late-model Mustang.

"Each car and each combination is unique. A suspension setup that works on one may not complement another, even though the two seem identical. There are no guarantees when it comes to the "right" suspension parts. . ."

the key to fine-tuning the whole enchilada. You'd be amazed at what can be done with a quality adjustable valving. Instead of altering spring rates side-to-side and asking for a bunch of other problems, adjust the shocks as a pair to compensate. A shock absorber works in two directions: compression (pushing it together), and rebound (pulling it apart). If the car heaves itself onto the right rear tire, adjusting the shocks so that the right rear pushes in harder and the left front pulls out harder will lessen or at least slow down that motion, just as if you'd put a stiffer spring on the right side. This requires quality adjustable shocks, such as the pricey Koni set. But if you're serious about maximum bite, consider them mandatory.

Each car and each combination is unique. A suspension setup that works on one may not complement another, even though the two seem identical. There are no guarantees when it comes to the "right" suspension parts, spring rates, shock valving, and so on. Gearing and clutch/converter are paramount when tuning the suspension, so the only way

to find out what works is by testing, testing, and more testing. It's expensive and time consuming, but mandatory for complete exploitation of the ubiquitous leaf spring suspension.

COIL SPRING SUSPENSIONS

If you are using a production coil spring car, you need a different plan of attack. These cars are notorious wheel hoppers. Two things must be done to control this hop. First, install a set of stiffer bushings in the control arms. Second, a set of air bags must be installed inside the coil springs. These air bags will actually stiffen up the coil spring and will provide equal traction to both tires. Due to the equal and opposite theory, the tires do not have equal forces on them. One is being planted and the other is trying to lift from the pavement. This is why a car will usually spin only the passenger side tire if it does not have a posi-traction rearend. The coil springs have the equal spring rates so their force is easily overcome. With the air

The front mounts of a four-link suspension. Four-link allows you to adjust the triangle, which on a ladder bar is set and immovable. How far forward you move the theoretical triangle is how much weight transfer you'll get.

bag installed, additional stiffness can be put into the passenger side spring and the traction can be equalized which should eliminate the wheel hop.

LINK SUSPENSION

If you have a faster car, you should consider some type of link suspension. These suspensions originated from the early '70s Pro stock race cars because they were having problems controlling the motion of their leaf springs. The two basic types of link sus-

pensions are the ladder bar and the four-link. Both use tubular bars or links to attach the rear end into the car. Because of this they can be infinitely adjusted for maximum traction. Both systems generally use a coil-over shock arrangement to support the vehicle and control its movement. Generally, they work perfectly but they will usually require professional installation and setup. If you are having a new car built, use one of these suspensions. After they are set up by the chassis shop, they will never need adjustment until you change power levels in the car. At this time, a new setup can be adjusted into the bars and it will again work perfectly. They will also allow a lower ride height than the more traditional production suspensions. However, they are only designed for going straight, so if your car sees street use, avoid the link suspension. Also, they are much more expensive than leaf or coil spring suspensions.

THE FRONT SUSPENSION

The front half of the car can do wonders for the back half's ability to hook up and get moving. A savvy hot rodder throws no parts at the engine without first considering the transmission and rearend. In a like manner of thinking, a quick launcher doesn't accommodate the rear suspension setup to the exclusion of the front. When a car comes off the line, the front end often lifts enough to pull the tires off the ground. That's good to a point because it puts the weight of the car on the rear tires. But once the front suspension runs out of travel or pulls the tires off the ground, lifting it any higher is only so much wasted motion. Because the rear wheels are already weighted at this point, you're using horsepower to lever the front when it really could be pushing the car forward. The dynamics of unsprung weight and travel, as well as spring rate and shock valving, determine the rate of front end lift.

Drag race coil springs are usually longer than normal but possess minimal rate. Low rate keeps the front end down and the extra length provides a lot of stored energy and a long duration of lift. When a travel limiter isn't used, the correct combination of coil spring and shock damping is the key to suspension control.

Stock front suspension parts are typically heavy. You can physically lift the front end of the car (old guys, and weaklings, or guys with bad backs—don't try this at home) a little because the stored energy in the coil springs is helping. The same thing happens as a car launches and the front end comes up. The springs help lift the car's front, at least until it's off the ground, but after that they're along for the ride, as are all the rest of the suspension components. The heavier these parts are, the harder it is for the engine to hoist them. The less unsprung weight (wheels, tires, brakes, spindles, and half the weight of the control arms) there is, the easier it is to lift the front of the car. That's why racers use lightweight brakes, skinny wheels, and thinly constructed tires.

The speed at which the front end lifts can be tailored by controlling the amount of front suspension travel. The springs help push the front end up until it runs out of suspension travel, at which point the tires come off the ground. A car that hooks really hard often lifts the front tires too high, but this can be cured by limiting suspension travel and removing the effect of the springs from the equation sooner. In other words, the front end comes up, suspension travel suddenly stops and produces enough of a shock load that the rise slows and the car moves forward. The harder the car leaves, the stiffer the front suspension needs to be. On a slick track or with a lower-powered engine, you may need a little help to get the nose in the air and the weight on the back tires, so extra travel and therefore more work from the springs is beneficial.

Suspension travel can be adjusted with a "limiter," and the rate of lift can be tuned with shock absorbers. The stiffer a shock is in rebound, the slower the front end will come up. With a 90/10 shock absorber, theoretically 90 percent of the dampening is in compression, and 10 per cent is in rebound. The piston extends nine times easier than it compresses, which lets the front end come up quickly and transfer weight to the rear tires, and then come down slowly to keep the weight back there.

Front suspension alignment is also a big concern. It doesn't do much for the launch, but it matters very much once the car is moving down the track. More caster gives the car greater stability at speed; to keep the tires pointed straight for minimal rolling resistance, camber and toe should be set at 0 degrees. Suspension travel, shock absorber settings, unsprung weight, and wheel alignment must always be considered when preparing for maximum performance. And

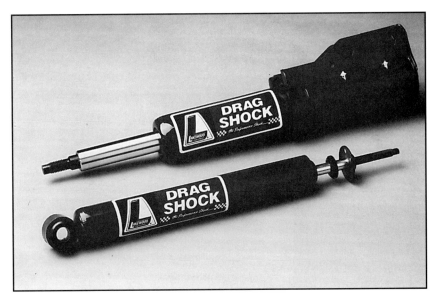

A typical 90/10 shock has more of its dampening in compression (bump) than in extension (rebound). An adjustable shock is even better, allowing the user to slow the rate of lift or quicken it, depending on track conditions. One caveat: Always make sure that suspension movement is stopped by the bumpstop or limiter, never the shock absorber. A shock with insufficient travel will stop the suspension and likely dislodge the piston from the housing.

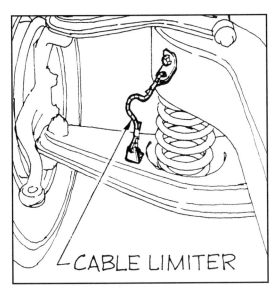

A cable or length of chain installed like this provides a crude yet effective limiter to control front end lift. Courtesy *Hot Rod* magazine.

"A properly prepared front end is no less important than the other primary systems. We'll bet there are a few tenths of a second or more hiding in the one in your car. "

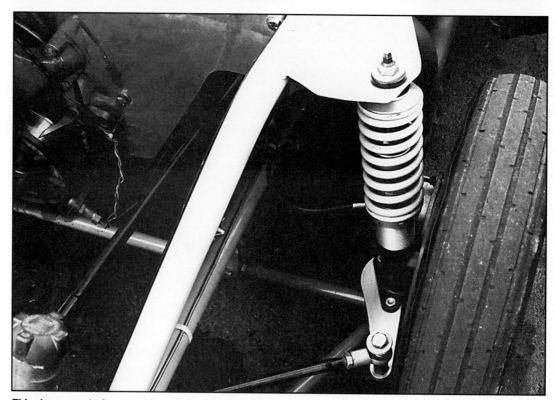

This drag racer's front end is stripped to the bare essentials. Reducing weight in the front of the car allows for a quicker rate of front end lift, which transfers the weight to the rear much quicker for improved traction during launch. Photo by Michael Lutfy.

Moving the battery rearward is one thing you can do to distribute more of the car's overall weight to the rear. There are many kits available for just about any application.

don't forget to use lightweight wheel bearing grease and minimize brake adjustment so that the wheels spin as freely as possible. If the entire package isn't taken into consideration, the car will never realize its potential. A properly prepared front end is no less important than the other primary systems. We'll bet there are a few tenths of a second or more hiding in the one in your car.

REDUCING WEIGHT

Weight also has a significant effect on suspension dynamics. Try to get the car as light as possible. It's easier to go faster by reducing weight than by increasing horsepower.

Let's quickly discuss the difference between sprung and unsprung weight. Unsprung weight is the weight that is exclusive of the suspension. The wheels, brakes and anything on the far side of the shock and springs is considered unsprung. You should run lightweight wheels—especially up front.

If rules allow for it, and you have some extra cash lying around, you can seriously reduce front end weight by opting for fiberglass replacements. This is a one-piece front end that offers a substantial savings in weight.

Lightweight wheels will reduce unsprung weight. Aluminum mags were developed more than just for show.

"If the car is going to be a track-only vehicle, eliminate as much weight as possible from the entire vehicle. If it's not essential, it's costing you ET."

Less weight on the front means quicker weight transfer to the rear and, hopefully, more adhesion. Distribution is also important. Try to keep as much weight on the rear as possible. This will increase traction. Shoot for 50-52% of total weight on the rear tires. See the sidebar on p. 73 for how to calculate your car's weight distribution. Using fiberglass front body panels will help as will relocating the battery into the trunk, preferably over the right tire. You may also want to remove the hood shield, or any insulation on the cowl or firewall (just for the run—put it back for driving home).

Lightweight wheels and tires also have a big effect on the car's ability to move quickly. This weight is unsprung weight, and as such, is more detrimental than sprung weight. Generally, if you save one pound of unsprung weight, it's like saving eight pounds of sprung weight. And you thought those fancy rims were for looks only! Invest in lightweight racing wheels and tires before buying any fiberglass other than a hood. If the car is going to be a track-only vehicle, eliminate as much weight as possible from the entire vehicle. If it's not essential, it's costing you ET.

If possible, reduce the weight on the wheels further by swapping your big heavy drum brakes for some drilled, milled discs. Or if that's not feasible, just look for alu-

Dual purpose tires, like those from **Mickey Thompson**, have soft sidewalls to allow for the wrinkling so conducive to traction, and a softer compound for stick. They are **DOT** approved, so you can drive them around town. However, they aren't designed for canyon running, so you may want to switch back to radials for running the twisties. If you are doing a lot of racing, you may want to keep a "race-only" set in the garage and put them on for the race weekend.

minum drums. Lots of older cars had them as OEM, you just have to find out which ones they were and then either get them used or buy replacements at the dealer. Again, brakes are a part of the unsprung weight and will hamper the suspension from doing what you wish to accomplish.

You can get plastic and fiberglass grilles to replace the OEM as well as even headlights of plastic which save just a few pounds. But overall, anything you do to reduce weight will help. The more you do the quicker the car will be. When you run, consider taking out the passenger and rear seats. Usually that can be accomplished by removing about eight bolts total and it shouldn't take more than just a few minutes.

By the way, don't drive to the track with a full gas tank. You still want to save the weight, remember. Doesn't matter that most fuel tanks are located over the rear wheels, you don't want extra weight.

TIRES

The best suspension in the world won't compensate for a combination of high torque and inadequate tires. On the street, the law specifies treaded, Department of Transportation–approved tires. Mickey Thompson, M&H, and BFGoodrich offer street tires that are quite effective, especially when the car owner knows how to tune the chassis for them. When it comes to slicks, the wider and taller they are, the better. A taller slick puts a bigger footprint on the ground, and that helps traction, but overall gear ratio must be considered.

Drag race tires are designed with a certain purpose in mind. Drag racing pro tires have soft walls, low pressure, and wrinkle when you tread on the throttle, then wind up and help launch the car. In addition, the soft sidewalls allow a larger footprint to be created, since the wheel is actually allowed to move

CALCULATING FRONT/REAR WEIGHT DISTRIBUTION

To find out the percentage of weight over your front wheels vs. your rear ones, you need to first weigh the car as accurately as possible. You should be able to find a public scale somewhere nearby (some tracks have them as well). They are also located at most moving companies. To be most accurate, weigh the car with all four wheels on the scale. Then, roll the car forward and take a reading with just the two rear wheels on the scale, then roll it back and weigh the front end. The addition of the two should equal the car's overall weight.

To find the percentage of weight on a given set of wheels, divide the weight on those wheels by the overall vehicle weight, and multiply the result by 100, or:

Wheel Weight Percentage = weight on wheels/overall weight x 100

For example, suppose you have a car that weighs 4000 pounds overall with 2240 pounds on the front wheels:

Wheel Weight Percentage = 2,240/4,000 x 100

The answer is 56 percent, which means that over one-half of the overall vehicle weight is located over the front wheels. If the scale were accurate, it would have shown 1760 pounds on the rear wheels.

Wheel Weight Percentage = 1,760/4,000 x 100

Or 44 percent. Of course, you could also have arrived at that figure by subtracting 56 from 100, but it wouldn't have been as much fun.

out and down as the tire winds up. It is strong, very light, relatively inexpensive (Goodyear charges about $250 per rear tire, which is a song compared to what they actually spend to make them), as adhesive as flypaper, and good for only a few runs.

The street tires you currently have on your car are a compromise at best. If your tires have tread, they're going to have less adhesion than a slick—which of course has no tread at all. Also consider the fact that today's tires are designed to last well over 50,000 miles. That's wonderful for the pocketbook, but not so great for the ET. You have to realize that the better the drivebility of any tire, the harder the rubber compound, meaning it will necessarily be less sticky. What you want is a tire that will perform well on the dragstrip, and for that, as we just mentioned, you want something very sticky and something that can wind up and help launch the car.

Don't make the mistake of reducing the air pressure in your street tires to six pounds and figure the walls will wrinkle, the tires will grab, and the car will shoot forward quicker than WJ's Oldsmobile. A radial tire, when underfilled, will tend to bend in the middle, so that the edges of the tires are on the ground, but the middle of the tire's tread doesn't even touch the pavement. So now, not only do you have a hard compound made for street application, you also have a tread design that reduces contact with the road, a set of sidewalls which don't wrinkle, no matter how little pressure you have in them, plus you now have the center of the tread that is bowed and doesn't touch the pavement.

But before you run off to buy new racing tires, realize that in some classes you don't have a choice; you have to run street tires. ■

TRACK TUNING

Your car will run differently from track to track, and even at different times of the day as weather and air conditions change. Being able to adapt to these conditions is the key to consistency, which is the key to winning bracket races. Photo by Michael Lutfy.

In this chapter you will be introduced to some ideas that have stood the test of time—as well as the average bracket racer's wallet.

First, as mentioned earlier, it isn't how fast you go, it's how you go fast. If your car can go a zillion mph, that's wonderful, but if you're constantly reacting to the Christmas Tree like a banana slug, then you're wasting your money on making your car fast. You'll never win, no matter how fast your car is. At the same time, if the car can go under 7 seconds, and your RT is great, none of it will matter if you can't tune the car for optimum conditions, unless you dial soft. But then, nothing is worse than spending all of the money for a car capable of running sevens (which costs thousands of dollars in high

Keeping a logbook with detailed notes of everything that happens during the course of the weekend is perhaps the most valuable tuning aid. Note weather and air conditions at different times of the day; log each run, or better yet, paste in every timeslip with a "run sheet" that includes tire pressure settings, track temperature, air temperature, time of day, etc. From this information, you can take some of the guesswork out of how the car will run under certain conditions.

"When you've run particularly well, take the time to painstakingly record what you did, so you can repeat it."

performance parts and substantial modifications) and having to run 10s or more because you can't tune it right.

Record Keeping

The best thing you can do is keep detailed records. Write down everything about your day at the track. What is the temperature? The humidity? How is the car going? How is the traction? What are the tire pressures before the run, and after? Where is the sun? What hour of the day is the race? How does it change from March to October?

Keeping accurate notes will improve your performance. You'll soon be able to pinpoint factors that affect your performance, and your consistency, good or bad. When you've run particularly well, take the time to painstakingly record what you did, so you can repeat it.

"But if you increase the density of the air, the more fuel you can burn and the greater the combustion, which means more power."

A big block needs big air. Make sure that you adjust the air/fuel mixture on your carbureted engine to adapt to changes in air density. Photo by Michael Lutfy.

NHRA's Pomona facility in California is host to the first and last race of the season. Because the track is at or near sea level, and the races are in January and October when the air is cool and dense, many records have been set at this track, usually at the end of the day. Photo by Michael Lutfy.

Changes in the track surface and changes in the air affect the performance of the car. If you don't write it down you'll have a tough time choosing the right setup to hit your dial-in.

WEATHER

As a drag racer, you're going to have to pay special attention to what the climate conditions are surrounding your race day. The difference between two tracks in two different locations and with two different climates can be the difference between being first or being the first eliminated.

Air Density

The greatest variable in any engine is the ability to process air. With normal pump fuel, you need twelve-and-a-half parts of air

Bernstein and his crew chief, Dale Armstrong, readily admit that Bandimere Raceway, about 5,000 feet above sea level, gives them headaches because of difficulties in tuning the engine. But the duo has no problem at sea level; along with many other records and championships, the duo were the first to crack 300 mph in Gainesville, Florida.

to one part of fuel (12.5 - 1) for combustion. That is a very important fact. No matter what you do, there is no way to change that ratio. You can adjust the compression ratio of the cylinders, adjust the air-fuel mixtures, compress the air, but you can still have no more than one part of fuel to twelve-and-a-half parts of air. But if you increase the density of the air, the more fuel you can burn and the greater the combustion, which means more power. How do you adjust for the air? First, you must understand what good air is. Like everything else in the world, air has weight. The density or weight of air is measured by the length of a column of mercury, measured in inches, the air can support. Ambient air pressure will support a column of mercury 29.9 inches, or roughly 14.7 pounds per square inch, at sea level. At 5,000 feet above sea level air is less dense than at sea level, and the air pressure is quite

different.

Now think of that difference in terms of your engine. If you run an engine at Pomona, California, home of the Winternationals and World Finals, then take the same car and run it at Bandimere Raceway, home of the Mile High Nationals in Denver, Colorado, without making any adjustments, there will be a disparity in performance. Some teams, like Kenny Bernstein's, have a tough time at Bandimere. Dale Armstrong, Bernstein's crew chief, has said he had never quite gotten the hang of running the car at peak performance at Bandimere.

The NHRA runs races from February through November, from the California coast to Colorado mountains, and from New Jersey humid to Arizona arid. But if you take a look at the history of Top Fuel in the United States, you'd find that almost every

"If you run an engine at Pomona, California, home of the Winternationals and World Finals, then take the same car and run it at Bandimere Raceway, home of the Mile High Nationals in Denver, Colorado, without making any adjustments, there will be a disparity in performance."

Cool, humid and dense air is optimum for peak performance, and Sears Point Raceway, located in Sonoma, California near the coast, delivers this type of air throughout most of the year.

top speed record is produced in one of only a few places: California, Texas, and Florida. This is because these tracks are located in areas with ideal atmospheric conditions.

The tracks in California that have produced top speeds are Pomona, Ontario, and Carlsbad, all at or near sea level. Most of the others have been in Texas, either outside Houston or Dallas, especially at the Texas Motorplex. True, in some cases, the track's actual construction (the 100-foot concrete launchpad at Texas is a big factor) has something to do with performances, but so does where it is located. Bandimere, is at 5,000 feet, and has not yet had a 300 mph pass (as of this writing) although they are commonplace in Top Fuel. Because the air is thinner, less fuel can be burned, which means less horsepower. Less horsepower means slower speeds.

Kenny Bernstein posted the first three hundred mile per hour run in Gainesville, Florida, in March of 1992. The weather was rainy off and on, with cool temperatures.

Florida, of course, is at sea level throughout most of the state. So Bernstein had a cool track and cool, dense air. During Friday's qualifying session, Bernstein and Armstrong stepped up to the plate and pulled out a 301.70, the fastest run in history.

Air Quality

"Good air," at least for racing, is cool, dense and wet. Cool air does not expand, making it more dense and heavier, and the more moisture there is the more oxygen there is available to burn. Dense air fills the cylinders more quickly with more oxygen and allows more fuel to burn and, of course, more fuel equals more power. Racers want wet, humid air, but not hot humid air. The heat makes the air expand and less dense. So the ideal conditions would be to run on a cool, foggy day at sea level; the worst is a hot, humid day at high altitude.

Reading Atmospheric Conditions

So the first question is, how do we know exactly what kind of air we have? The next is, how do we adjust the engine to compensate for it?

Of the three factors involved in figuring atmospheric conditions—temperature, altitude, and air density—temperature is the most crucial. Although the engine will produce more power and run more efficiently if its components are warmed up, it still needs cool air for peak efficiency. This is why engineers try to separate the air intake from the rest of the engine compartment as much as possible, to try to keep the air cool. That hot air will drop horsepower very quickly.

If you are traveling to a local track, check to see what the temperature will be, getting the high and low, whether it is expected to be cloudy or sunny. Call the weather bureau in your area and get a reading, if possible. Find out the temperature and the relative humidity. If rain appears likely in the next couple of days you will do things differently than if it is hot and sunny. Similarly, if you're leaving for the track at 4:00 p.m. and will be racing into the evening, remember that the air will be cooling—actually, improving—as the evening wears on, making it more dense.

To accurately read the atmospheric conditions, you'll need barometer (air pressure), a thermometer (temperature), and an altimeter (altitude).

Altitude—The first reading you need to take is altitude. The higher the dragstrip is above sea level the thinner the air. The thinner the air, the less oxygen there is to burn with the air/fuel mixture. When you have less oxygen, you have a smaller bang in the cylinder.

Relative Humidity—Another factor that changes the setting of the car is relative humidity. Humidity is the amount of water present in the air. Excessive humidity is not necessarily a bad thing unless the water within the air is hot. And as long as humidity is not 100 percent, the engine will likely run well—certainly better than in a situation with low relative humidity. Of course, if you have a humid day and it's hot, all bets are off. The heat will change the effect the humidity has.

Having said all that, there's a gizmo that can give you a better read on temp, humidity, and altitude. It's a density altitude instrument. What it does is calculate corrected altitude based on temperature, humidity or density, and altitude. What that means essentially is that it gives you a kind of abstract reading that compares in ideal situations to a run at a certain sea level. It really correlates to a situation which would be equivalent to about 30 inches on the barometer and about 55-60 degrees. So going from track to track, you get a corrected altitude but you don't mess around much with the temp and air density.

Let's say your car runs 10.00s at a corrected altitude of 100 feet, but then in the afternoon it runs 10.20 seconds and your readout shows that the corrected altitude on that day

is 2,100 feet, which is very possible—especially at someplace that changes as rapidly as Sears Point. Realize that for a 2,000 foot change the car has changed roughly 1/100th

Here's an almost essential tuning aid: a portable weather station. These three gauges give readouts in temperature, barometric pressure and relative humidity.

The state of the art is this little handheld density altitude meter, which gives you corrected altitude based on current atmospheric conditions.

Carbureted engines are tuned by changing jet sizes to regulate the air/fuel mixture. To "lean" out an engine means to add less fuel, something you would do if the air was hot, dry, and at high altitude (less air, less fuel). Conversely, if the air is cool and dense, meaning there's more of it packing into the cylinders, then you want to run "rich" with more fuel to compensate. Photo by Michael Lutfy.

Colorado, you can sometimes get corrected altitudes of 10,000 feet. That's why engines blow up and nobody can get their cars dialed in.

Compensating for Weather

What we're getting at here is that you need to constantly monitor the weather to adjust your dial in. Because bracket racing is a game of hundredths of a second, very minute changes in density and temperature can be the difference between breaking out or getting the win light. In your notebook, you should note the temperature, relative humidity, air pressure, or the corrected altitude if you can (if you don't have these instruments, you might find a friendly competitor to give you the readings).

If you know that the track is going to get warmer at a certain time of the day, and you have a baseline set up from the previous week, then when it moves up in temperature that should mean your practice time will be just slightly slower. You may not be able to get an instant indication of what's about to happen, but you can determine your dial-in from just a few runs.

As the track cools in the evening, be ready to adjust your standard dial-in downward; your car will be quicker. Say your car ran a 21.16, then a 21.15, then a 21.13. Your records indicate that at night, the car runs 21.10s pretty consistently. Make sure you dial-down accordingly.

Now let's say it's really hot. One of those Southern nights, where everyone is outside on the porch fanning themselves and talking about how hot it is, wondering if they can take it anymore. And it's not getting any cooler. Now your first run is a 21.34, then a 21.35, then a 21.40. If everything else checks out, chances are the culprit is the heat and change in the corrected altitude. The rest of the field should be having the same problem. Adjust your dial-in accordingly or perhaps re-jet your carburetor (if so equipped)

for each hundred feet of corrected altitude. That's a big difference and if you aren't paying attention to it, you'll be left in the dust if you did everything exactly the same down to the thousandths of a second with the car prepared as perfectly as it can be at different corrected altitudes.

By the way, the corrected altitude can and does change radically through an average day. It can be zero, two hundred feet below zero, or in the afternoons, at places which tend to be very hot in the summer, it can read three thousand feet above sea level. If you can imagine a very hot afternoon in July in

This device monitors the air/fuel mixture and compensates accordingly. The "STO" on the label is for "stoichiometric," which is the ideal air/fuel ratio of 14.7:1.

If you can't or don't feel like tuning the engine, change your dial-in to compensate. If the air has deteriorated, you can bet that you're going to run slower, so give yourself some additional cushion. In most cases, you can change right up until you get to the tower.

"Some drivers will take last week's dial-in and leave it there through the month. But in order to race each and every time to win, you need to complete your due diligence and keep adjusting your dial-in."

to compensate.

In the final analysis, you still have to do some homework when you bracket race. Some drivers will take last week's dial-in and leave it there through the month. But in order to race each and every time to win, you need to complete your due diligence and keep adjusting your dial-in.

TIRE PRESSURES

Along with your log book and pen, your mini weather station and cool gauges, you should get a tire gauge. That doesn't mean one of those plastic silver things that looks like a pen. Trying to adjust tire pressures for drag racing with one of those is not the best way to go. You're better off getting a professional type gauge that has a needle gauge in 1 pound increments. Tire pressure is criti-

"*Then you go and have the tires back on hot asphalt for up to an hour or so in staging, then burnout. Your tire pressure by the end of the run may have increased by as much as 20 psi!*"

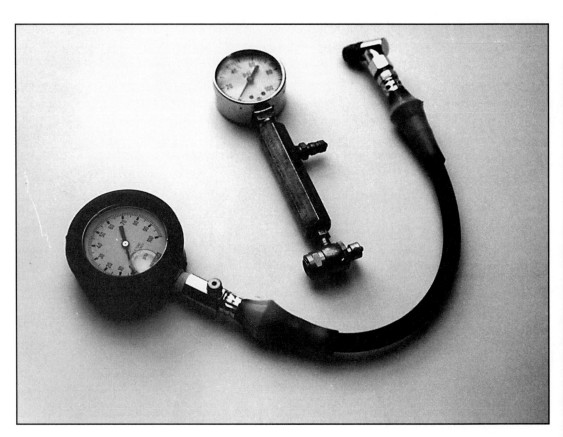

You must invest in a professional quality tire gauge. If you can afford it, get a liquid filled unit. Photo by Michael Lutfy.

cal—probably one of the most critical aspects of performance in drag racing. If the tires are overinflated, the tire will bulge out and there will be less of a "footprint," the contact patch with the ground. If the tires are underinflated, you will increase the rolling resistance, which can slow you down.

Setting Tire Pressures—You may figure that all you need to do is follow the manufacturer's recommended specs. Set the tires to the number on the sidewall, and leave it at that. But what you are not figuring on is the increase in tire pressure that will result from heat. This is particularly true if you do a burnout, but even it you don't do one, the track and ambient temperatures can also have a significant effect.

If you set the temps in the morning, when the tires are cold, and the temperature is mild (say around 50 degrees) by afternoon, as the temperature increases to where it is very hot (around 80 degrees), the tire pres-

sure will also increase. Then you go and have the tires back on hot asphalt for up to an hour or so in staging, then burnout. Your tire pressure by the end of the run may have increased by as much as 20 psi!

How do you adjust for this? The only way is through testing and record keeping. To get a baseline, set tire pressures to the recommended setting, note the track and ambient temperature. While you're in the staging lanes, particularly if it's for a long period of time, check the pressures to see if they have risen at all during the heat and make a note of it. Then, make your run, then check the pressures after the run (do this for all four tires, by the way), immediately back at the pit. It should be one of the first things you do.

To adjust your tire pressure, you will need to set them lower to compensate for the increase. However, don't just figure that if they increased four pounds by the end of the they increased four pounds by the end of the run, that you need to set them four pounds lower. You'll need to factor in the ambient temperature and the track conditions, and whether or not you performed a burnout, and for how long. This is a perfect example of why you need to develop a routine. Varying the length of your burnout will also vary your tire pressures. A burnout of 1 minute vs. 30 seconds will make a big difference in heat.

Tire Profiles—The wrong pressure will give your tire a profile that may reduce its traction. Serious racers spend good money on very precise tire gauges to make sure they keep the tire in the same shape every time they go to the line, and you should consider it too.

When setting pressures, you have to also consider just how much you want them inflated, and for what purpose. A tire that is slightly overinflated will have less contact with the road and therefore less rolling resistance, which is what you want with your front tires. Grip is not nearly as important as it is for the rear. For the rears, the opposite is true, but only to a point. You want to strike a balance between maximum adhesion and underinflation. You don't want the tires to be too underinflated as to be unsafe (consequently, you don't want to overinflate the fronts to the point where they will be unsafe, either). By the way, remember to adjust your tire pressures to the recommended street settings at the end of the day if your race car is going to be driven home. ■

> "This is a perfect example of why you need to develop a routine. Varying the length of your burnout will also vary your tire pressures. A burnout of 1 minute vs. 30 seconds will make a big difference in heat."

You must determine the optimum tire pressure setting for your run. To do so means setting them lower than the desired pressure, to compensate for a rise in pressure caused by the burnout and the run. Track temperature, and time spent in staging area (during hot weather) is a factor. In general, you will often set them lower than you would for driving on the street. If that is the case, then remember to fill them back up before you drive home. Photo by Michael Lutfy.

After you get the hang of running, it's time to focus on honing your technique to produce winning results. Photo by Michael Lutfy.

Bracket racing is one of the only motorsports where a racer can lose by actually getting to the finish line first. It is also a difficult sport to win at consistently because there are so many ways to lose. As discussed earlier, if a racer goes faster than his posted dial-in or leaves the line before the green light, he will lose the race. Although the strategy can be a factor in bracket racing, being consistent and doing everything the same each and every time is really the way to win bracket races. I will illustrate some strategies to help increase your winning percentage. Try to enjoy the ride and keep the games to a minimum. Don't psyche yourself out of the race while you are trying to psyche out your opponent! Remember that you are racing the

Once you get into the staging lanes, it's time to put on your "race face." Focus on the start, how you are going to stage, run over your routine. Concentration is important.

"But if you truly want to be successful, you have to treat it more than just a "weekend at the beach" type of recreational affair. You must learn to keep your emotions in check and focus on tuning and driving the car."

clock, not your opponent. Be a machine while you are driving, focused on one thing only: driving consistently.

Concentrate

From the moment you get into the gate until the instant you leave the track, your mind will be wandering, planning, and thinking about things other than racing. Often, the most difficult thing to concentrate on is, oddly enough, racing itself. Professional racers must learn to control their emotions.

When you go to professional races and cruise the pits, whether it is NHRA National events or Indycars or NASCAR, you will observe that the drivers often are very serious, detached, and somewhat tense. What they are is focused. From the moment they arrive at the track until they leave, they are in "the racing mode." Most people who are successful in motorsport have sufficiently desensitized themselves to the emotion behind this sport that they look less than overjoyed by the whole process of winning.

In fact, that's exactly what it is, a part of the process. Winning is just the final step in a long involved collection of duties the pro driver must accomplish.

The idea is not to make this boring; just less emotional. You want to enjoy what you're doing, because bracket racing is fun. But if you truly want to be successful, you have to treat it more than just a "weekend at the beach" type of recreational affair. You must learn to keep your emotions in check and focus on tuning and driving the car.

For example, if you come to the line and you are not completely focused, you will certainly lose your edge. This is a sport of big horsepower, but very small numbers. If you are not on your game, you will lose— maybe by just a few thousandths of a second, but you will still be eliminated from competition and the other guy, the guy who was paying attention, will advance.

Most other types of racers have the luxury of making a mistake or suffering a momentary lapse in concentration, because they often have plenty of time to recover during

Looking at this picture, you'd never know that this guy is next to be waved up to the burnout box. Elbows in, focus and get ready. That doesn't mean you have to "white knuckle" the wheel, but at least concentrate and focus.

This laid-back style may be fine for cruising your favorite main strip, but it is hardly conducive to car control and racing. Move the seat upright and closer than you would for normal driving. You'll have more control.

the course of a one, two or three hour race. Drag racers don't. You get one shot, and if you are slow at the line, or don't keep it straight and have to lift, you will likely lose unless the other guy makes a bigger mistake.

If this happens during the first round, it makes for a very short weekend.

Of course, not concentrating can have consequences far more serious than just losing the race. Making a mistake at well over 100 mph can certainly be fatal. All the more reason to pay attention.

So the first step is to free your mind from peripheral outside influences. Now is not the time to be arguing with your girlfriend or wife. Don't be going over the project for work the next day, or stressing over an argument with your boss. Many racers employ deep breathing techniques, taking a few moments of quiet time in the rig or even inside the car during staging, to deep breathe, relax and clear the mind.

DRIVER POSITION

One item rookie bracket racers frequently overlook is their seating position. Climb into the car, and assess where and how you are sitting. Many drag racers mistakenly believe the best position is to recline the seat slightly and lean back, extending their arms out in front of them, elbows locked. But this classic driving position really doesn't give enough control. In Driver's Ed high school class you're taught to place your hands at the two and ten positions, but what you should do in racing is place your hands at the nine and three positions on the wheel, move your seat up a notch or two until your knees are slightly bent. Adjust the rake of the seatback until your elbows are bent, and that the shifter, if it is on the console, is right at hand as you lower it. You shouldn't have to reach much for it at all.

To test the distance, put both feet on the pedals, make sure your shoulder blades touch the back of the seat and then move your hands over the wheel. If you can touch all parts of the wheel with the middle of the palm of your hand, you're fine. But if you need to move your shoulder blades off the seatback or have to use your fingers or fin-

This racer is ready to race. He's sitting upright, both hands on the wheel, checking his dial-in before staging. His chances of winning have just gone up.

ger tips, you're too far back.

Winston Cup stock car drivers sit with the steering wheel right next to their chest. They found that when wrestling with a car for four hours, this position gives them more leverage to move the wheel. So move the seat up a notch or two. Not as far as the NASCAR guys, but just a bit forward from normal until your elbows and knees are slightly bent. When you leave the track, return the seat to the position you are most comfortable in.

BURNOUTS

Many racers consider the burnout not only necessary, but a lot of fun. Having a legitimate excuse for burning rubber, without getting nailed by the cops, is almost too much to resist. Just like the pros you've seen at national events. The main purpose of a burnout is to heat the tires to get the surface rubber "sticky" for maximum traction, and, if you're tuning this way, to increase your tire pressure to the desired setting.

But at many tracks, there are signs that say, "No Burnouts With Street Tires." Part

of the reason for this is that the tread can track water from the water box up to the starting line, or the tread may discard too much rubber debris, or scuff the rubber patch that is already on the track surface.

Another reason you may not want to do a burnout is that most street cars have no lim-

Some tracks may not allow burnouts for certain classes. Remember, the purpose is to scrub the tires clean and heat them up for additional traction—not to see how much smoke you can produce.

Wait for the burnout director to signal you forward, then wait until he tells you to go ahead and light 'em up. Don't be a rookie and stick your head out the door to look at all the smoke. Keep both hands on the wheel, and be prepared if the car starts to slide (middle). If one wheel grabs suddenly, it could shoot the car forward at an angle, catching you off guard. Lift off the throttle immediately if you can't correct for this. Middle & Bottom photos by Michael Lutfy.

ited slip differential. That means that as you stomp the pedal, only one wheel will spin. You've got one tire that has a consistency of hot bubble gum and one that is stone cold and hard. If you develop problems down the track, you will have one tire that is very hot and three that are cold. Talk about poor traction, does it make sense to have three of the four tires at different temperatures, and one tire sticky and pliable? Not really.

Proper Technique

Be ready when the staging director motions you to move forward to the burnout box. If you are on street tires, make sure you drive around the deep trough of water in the box, then back up to the damp part of the burnout box. If you're on slicks, roll forward through the puddle of water, which is in a dip, then wait for the man in charge of the burnout box, or the starter, to signal that it is okay for you to begin your burnout. Do not try to a burnout until you are told. Engage the line lock if so equipped, or if not, tap the brakes (assuming you're driving an automatic, if not, depress the clutch, hit the brakes), wait for the front end to dip, and at the same moment rev the engine. With your right foot planted firmly on the throttle and your left foot on the brake the tires should begin to spin. If not, keep the throttle planted and release the brake slightly, then mash your foot on the brake again to try to bring the front end down and the rear end up. Eventually the rear tires—or tire—should spin.

When performing the burnout, do not open the door and look out the back to see if the tires are spinning, or to see how cool all that smoke looks. Keep your eyes focused straight ahead, both hands on the steering wheel, ready to correct if the tires should start to grab or if the car starts to dance sideways. Quite often, during a burnout, the car will start to get sideways, and the outside tire will suddenly have traction, shooting the car unexpectedly forward at an angle. If you

Do not carry your burnout across the start finish line, like you see in the pros. Those guys can do it, you will only irritate the starter (mainly because it takes too much time to back up, then creep forward, etc. By the way, this photo also illustrates what you get on a car without a limited slip differential— a one-wheeled burnout.

aren't ready for this, you could be in trouble. Be prepared to get out of the throttle immediately.

One final thing: in the pros, you may have seen them burnout all the way across the start/finish line, with a big cloud of smoke. But if you do that in brackets, you may really upset the starter and find yourself heading home earlier than you thought.

STAGING TECHNIQUES

Previous chapters touched on staging, but now it will be explained in detail—what it is and what you can do to make it work for you. But before you do any of this, check to see if the track has a policy of some sort. Many tracks employ a courtesy rule, that means the first car into the lights must wait until the second car is prestaged before fully staging. Starters do this to eliminate the following psyche games, mainly in the interest of time. When you have 600 bracket cars in a single weekend, things have to be kept moving along.

As discussed earlier, when you move the car forward, you pass in front of a light beam, which will trigger the first amber lights on the top of the Christmas Tree. These are the pre-stage lights. As you move forward again you pass before another beam, the staging light, which electronically

Most of the time, starters will not allow staging games at the bracket level. They've got to move things along, and generally won't allow deep or late staging. Move up and stage quickly when the starter tells you to do so. If you don't, and he thinks you're playing games, he may just give you a redlight.

Here's one of the dangers of late staging. At top, the Nova is slow getting to the line, while the Camaro is already waiting to go (top). But when the Nova finally gets there, the starter is in no mood, and hits the button right away. You can see in bottom photo that the Camaro has pulled a holeshot on the Nova, most likely because he was ready, while the Nova was playing around. Photos by Michael Lutfy.

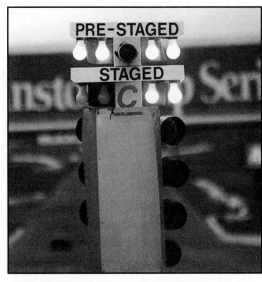

The guy on the right is staged, ready to go, but the guy on the left is hanging back. This is late staging.

triggers the two amber lights directly beneath the pre-stage lights. You have now signaled the starter that you are ready to race.

Here's where the games begin, and you need to decide if you want to play. Some people prefer to use the staging lights as a kind of psychological game. They pre-stage and then wait until you pre-stage and then wait again as you stage before they make the final move. Sometimes it is effective. And sometimes it irritates the starter. Races are often won and lost on psychology like that. But most racers feel that if you play games, you are subject to losing them.

Using tricks like these are usually ineffective in the pro classes. Sure, in Pro Stock they sometimes wait so long between pre-staging and staging that they try to actually burn their opponent down by making them overheat. A good starter will stop that from

happening by red-lighting a slow stage. But for the most part pros are immune from that kind of nonsense. They are not as concerned with their opponent as they are with themselves, which is what you should be concerned with too. Focus on what you are doing not what your opponent is doing.

In that respect, most good drag racers come to the line, do stage quickly and wait for the starter to hit that button. Once they do their only job is to race down the lane. But you should be familiar with these techniques in case they are ever used against you.

Late Staging

Late staging would go something like this: You've done a huge burnout and pre-stage first. The guy in the Dodge next to you follows. You wait. He waits. He stages. You wait. And wait. Finally, thinking you're the coolest guy on the line, you stage too... and the starter, who is pretty irritated with your shenanigans, smacks the button the second your stage light is lit, as if he's the one trying to cut a perfect light, catching you completely off guard.

Have there been instances where drivers have been psyched out by that kind of stupid stuff? Certainly. In fact, most drivers have at

some time or another. But what did you learn from this example? The guy in the Dodge was prepared. He had done his business and was now staged and concentrating on the light. You, on the other hand, were playing the waiting game, and thinking about that, not about racing. Once you did decide to move forward you had several things to worry about: first, you had to worry about how far forward to roll to trigger the stage light; then you had to worry about stopping the car and then, finally, you had to worry about the race. Then the starter goes and starts the race before you were ready. It makes more sense to be ready in the first place, without all the games.

Deep Staging

First, a definition of what deep staging is: As already mentioned, staging and pre-staging is done by a set of lights. But the timing for your elapsed time will actually begin as you move out of the stage beam or, at some tracks, forward into the "start ET light," which is a few feet ahead of the stage beam.

If you roll all the way through the stage light, the pre-stage light will actually go out. It's a kind of mental advantage, not to mention the physical advantage which has you out front even before the race starts. Although you are only a few extra inches ahead of your opponent, your opponent knows it, and in some cases, it will have affected his or her concentration.

There are a couple of problems with deep staging, however. First is the fact that the deep stage leaves some room for interpretation as to where you are on the race track. It is difficult to do it the same way every time. Remember that the key to bracket racing is to be consistent.

Another problem is that when you deep stage, you use all of the available rollout space, so it is easier to red-light. There is about a foot and a half before the stage light will go out and trigger the Start ET light—less, if the track used the unblocking of the stage light as the way to begin timing the ET. Deep staging, in essence, moves you six inches closer to the finish line. In a game of hundredths of a second, it can make a slight difference. With a running start, you can

At left, you can tell if your opponent has deep staged if the pre-stage light goes out, while the stage light remains lit. At right, both of these guys have deep staged, trying to gain an advantage of about six inches to a foot. The problem with deep staging is that you use all of the available rollout, increasing your chances for a red-light.

Whatever staging strategy you eventually adopt, make sure you do it consistently. Try to put the car in exactly the same spot each and every time. Photo by Michael Lutfy.

leave a few fractions of a second early. But if you are already closer to beginning your run—that is, to starting the ET clock running—than your opponent, it means you have to allow that extra moment before you can plant your foot in the throttle. The difference is extremely slight, but it does exist, and with a deep stage start you may find yourself cutting the light too quickly. If you consistently deep stage, you'll learn to leave at the appropriate time more frequently, but you will never completely alleviate the problem. The closer you get to the start ET light the less room there is for error.

So remember, if you plan on deep staging, you must be consistent and deep stage every time.

You might try it during practice runs to see if it suits you. But remember, it is a wasted day in terms of dialing your car in for the next weekend should you decide you don't like deep staging. Veteran bracket racers will be trying to fine tune their car from week to week depending on air temps and track conditions. You will be fiddling with deep stag-

ing as well as all that other stuff. Who do you think will do better in the long run?

Bear in mind that some tracks don't even allow it. If you get to the line and there is a blue light on the Tree, that means deep staging in not allowed. Some tracks and some classes prohibit the practice of deep staging and will red-light you before you even begin. Certainly you can prevent that from happening, but again, if you are striving to be consistent and have adopted deep staging as part of your technique and you then go to a track which doesn't allow deep staging, you will need every practice around to figure a decent dial-in as opposed to using the prelims for getting the car tuned for the day and the track. You're behind again.

Stage Consistently

Along with being consistent on late or deep staging, as discussed above, you should also try to put the car into the staging beams at the same spot each time. This is very hard to do, but it gets easier with practice. By trying to do this, you will have more

Some people will react to the Tree much quicker as the sun goes down. If you find this is true, and you are using a delay box, then you will want to change your RT setting to compensate.

consistent reaction times since you are leaving from the same spot each time. Also, remember that the roll out may be different from lane to lane and may require some slight adjustments to keep the reaction times in the ballpark. Always keep track of these things and record them in your logbook. This is especially important if you travel around to different tracks.

THE START

The next area to concentrate on is the start itself. Establish a particular routine, position, breathing technique, whatever, and stay

with it. If you like to do a burnout first and stage last, do it each and every time. This is all a part of being consistent. Don't let your opponent try to intimidate you into breaking your concentration.

Fiddling With RT

If you are using a delay box, try to resist the temptation to change the setting based on your opponent at the line. If you have been cutting .520 lights all afternoon, don't risk red-lighting by taking some time out of the box just because the track champ is staged in the lane next to you and you know he is going to drop a .501 light on you. Remember that a .499 light is a loser! The only time you should change the box setting is to compensate for different roll outs from lane to lane or for changing lighting conditions. Some people will actually react to the Tree faster as the sun goes down and it gets darker. Practice will be the best teacher for this to see how you react. See page 101 for tips on improving your RT skills. Again, take some notes and write them down for future reference.

Launching

Since one car will usually leave first, some strategy will come into play as the race is being run. Many people consider the faster car (which leaves last) to have the advantage during the race. This is due to three main reasons.

First, the faster driver can see the other car the whole way down the track. This allows the faster driver to judge the closing gap more accurately than the slower driver. The slower driver has to look in his mirrors to judge the oncoming car and still concentrate on keeping his car straight; it's distracting.

Second, the slower car has the disadvantage of having the first chance to red-light. There can only be one red-light loser. If the first car has a red-light, the other car can leave before the green and still win the race. However, remember the "first or worst" rule

"Many people consider the faster car (which leaves last) to have the advantage during the race. This is due to three main reasons."

"If you are easily intimidated, consider taking up a new hobby. You are absolutely capable of winning regardless of speed difference because this is bracket racing."

The truck gets to leave first in this handicapped start (he's dialed in at 13.50 while his opponent is dialed in at 12.16), putting him at a slight disadvantage, because he'll have to keep looking over his shoulder while trying to focus on keeping the car straight.

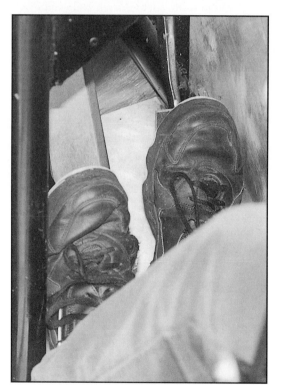

Adopt a left-foot braking technique for starting. It's not recommended for driving on the street, but on the track you'll save the time spent moving one foot off the brake to the throttle. Every fraction counts.

of thumb discussed earlier. If the first car red-lights (first infraction) but the second car crosses the center line or spews engine oil all over the track as an engine lets go (worse infraction), the first car is actually the winner, because the red-light is not considered as bad as crossing the center line. Don't count on this rule to save you from losing, as red-light reversals are very rare.

The third disadvantage to leaving first comes from intimidation by the faster car. Face it, if your opponent has a shiny new, low-slung, seven second car, he is going to smoke the doors off your 15-second street car. If you are easily intimidated, consider taking up a new hobby. You are absolutely capable of winning regardless of speed difference because this is bracket racing. Don't admit defeat before the race begins.

Left Foot Braking & Shifting

Assuming you don't have any electronic aids, which are discussed in Chapter 5, let's go over the actual physical technique of launching off the line. The quickest method is to use one foot on the brake and one foot on the gas. Left foot braking, as it's known, is much more efficient and gives far more control. Moving the right foot from brake to gas is incredibly slow in a world defined by hundredths of seconds.

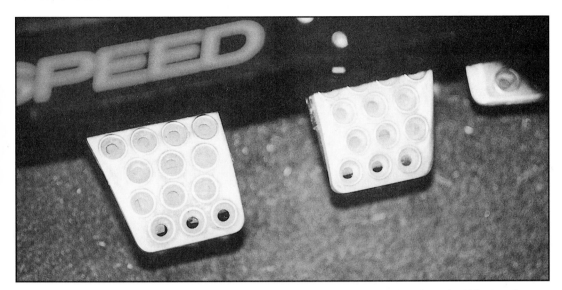

If you're rowing your own gears, you'll have to employ some fancy footwork to launch. Side-stepping the clutch is not necessary. You can add these extra wide pads that offer more contact surface and grip.

"If you miss a shift by 200 rpm, you have missed your dial-in."

A common mistake while driving an automatic is to shift the car manually—that is, go from 1 to 2 to 3 or 4 if it has a fourth that isn't an overdrive. But most serious racers who use a street car equipped with an automatic say the best way to shift is to let the transmission do it all by itself. Not that the car will go faster (although that might be the case), but that the automatic is much more consistent. If you miss a shift by 200 rpm, you have missed your dial-in. It's easier to take one more variable out of the process and let the transmission do what it is already designed to do.

Manual Transmission—If you're driving a car with a manual transmission, you will be at the mercy of the clutch operation and your left foot. For the most part there isn't a great deal you can do here except use a line lock, then go up in revs with the clutch just to the point of engagement. Automatic is definitely the way to go in drag racing. But if you have a manual transmission car and want to race it, you will have to know the exact instant the clutch releases and the pressure plate grabs the flywheel. The other thing is that unless you use the line lock you will have no brake. It seems remarkable that on a track which is calibrated to be flat that you can actually roll away from the starting

line, but it actually can happen. But hopefully it is flat and you can come off the gas, let the clutch out to the point where it's trying to get away and when the green light comes on, engage it quickly. No reason to blow something up by side stepping it. Lift off the clutch to the point of engagement, let it slip briefly, then release your foot entirely. Of course, try to do it the same each time

The most efficient way is to use the handbrake if the car has a tendency to roll, slipping it off when the light comes on. Or what some drivers do is a sort of modified heel and toe (by the way, if you know how to do the classic heel and toe, this isn't it). They use their heel on the brake and their toes on the throttle and when they leave they simply sidestep the brake.

Lane Selection

Another area where starting strategy comes into play is lane selection. Funny Car legend John Force eyeballs the track really well before going down it. He lies on his stomach, and puts his cheek to the ground. Although he keeps the information to himself, he must have something there, because at this writing he's posted his sixth Funny Car title.

Although you may not be racing for the

The only way you get to choose your lane at the bracket racing level is to line up in the staging area accordingly. Once you get to the staging area director, shown above, you must go where he tells you. You can't just cross over to the next lane. Think ahead, and plan accordingly. Photo by Michael Lutfy.

Dick LaHaie, former NHRA Top Fuel Champion and the engineer of a pair of Top Fuel Championships for Scott Kalitta, checks the track for conditions. Pros usually check the launch area prior to each run, and monitor lanes to see which one is posting faster times and wins (if any). If you're a serious bracket racer, you should adopt similar strategies.

stakes that Force is, you still want to know the inconsistencies between the lanes. Reading the track the way Force does may not be practical or possible. Most tracks won't allow you to be at the starting line unless you are in your car. But what you can do is take a run in each lane during practice. Make sure you have done that sometime before the elimination rounds. If you run the same RTs and same ETs then you know the lanes are pretty similar for your car. If not then make a note of it and remember which lane does what and where it happens, if you know. Observe other drivers and racers, and see if there is any pattern to consistent times and wins between lanes. If the right lane is producing more consistent times and winners, then maybe there is more traction, or something else. Perhaps one lane has far more red-lights, which could mean the roll-out area is shorter, and drivers aren't compensating for it.

Lane selection is usually determined by where you happen to be parked when you come to staging, but it will also be sorted out by the Racemaster or Staging Director as you come to the line. The Racemaster is the guy who stands ahead of the starter, and who motions you forward from the burnout box or from behind staging. He calls the numbers on your windshield to the tower by radio if they can't be read by the people in the tower (figuring there is a tower; it might be just a trailer or a booth).

How you make your lane choice is based on where you park. It's usually as simple as that. Once in line, you can't back up and move over, you can't switch with the guy next to you and you can't pass on the race. Once you've parked you've made a selection and you're pretty much stuck with it, so choose carefully.

Before you stage, check your dial-in to make sure the tower or starter has gotten it right. Typos do happen! Once you stage, you are accepting the dial-in and you cannot change it. The dial-in will either be displayed at the top end on the scoreboard, or on an LED display near the starting line.

Now if everybody knows that one lane is better than the other and the entire field lines up in one lane, the track officials are going to have to sort this situation out. Somebody there will end up in the bad lane. Sometimes you have a choice, sometimes you don't.

DIAL-IN STRATEGIES

You always have the ability to move your dial-in up or down at any time while waiting in staging lanes. Even up to the last minute before you go to the burnout box, you can change the figure you have on your windshield.

However, before you stage at the starting line, make sure you look at the finish line scoreboards (or wherever they are displayed—sometimes they are displayed on LED readouts near the starting line) to check your handicap dial-in. If your dial-in is displayed incorrectly, STOP! Wave to the starter for a correction. Once you have staged, your dial-in is locked in and you

"If you find yourself against a much faster car, always dial tight and run it all out. Don't even look back because you won't see anything until it's too late to react."

Some guys dial-in "loose" or "soft" and get out of the throttle or hit the brakes on the top end just an instant before they get to the finish line to fool or confuse their opponent. This is called "dumping." Because it is hard to do consistently, you shouldn't make it standard practice. Also, dumping can backfire on you. You may be so worried about the guy behind you that you forget to lift at the end, and break out. Photo by Michael Lutfy.

have accepted it, even if the tower made the mistake. You may be running in a bracket your car is not capable of!

Some racers use their dial-in time to establish some strategy for the race. If you are the slower car, you may want to dial your car "tight" or "hard." This means that you are going to dial the car in with its fastest time of the day and run it flat out each time. Conversely, some people dial their car in "loose" or "soft," and get out of the throttle or hit the brakes (called *dumping*) just an instant before the finish line to fool their opponent. Sometimes this can work but more often than not, it backfires because it can't be done consistently. If your car has run 11.36 and you dial soft and put 11.39 on the car with the intention of dumping at the finish line, you may break out if you mis-

judge the other car. This is especially true if the other car is much faster than yours. If you dial in soft with the 11.39 and you are racing a dragster with a 8.19 dial in, the dragster is going to go flying by you at the end so fast that you won't even know where it came from, let alone accurately judge their skinny front tire. In this situation, you will keep looking back for the other car. Since you can't see it at all, you stay in the throttle until the end. Unfortunately for you, your car will run its flat out ET of 11.36 and you lose by a break out. In this situation the dragster "pushed you out" by forcing you to break out. Don't let this happen.

If you find yourself against a much faster car, always dial tight and run it all out. Don't even look back because you won't see anything until it's too late to react. This is a com-

The dragster dialed-in at an 8.85, nearly 2 seconds faster than the altered. The altered guy should be dialed-in as tightly as possible and run flat out without looking back.

mon mistake, especially with beginning racers, and it's part of the reason that dragsters are so successful in bracket racing. They are usually fast and they are very hard to judge. Generally it's best to dial tight and run your own race each time. Let the other person make the mistake and give you the win light.

Real World

Now let's try to tie all of these concepts—dial-in, elapsed time, reaction time, starting technique etc.—into a concrete example. What follows is a typical scenario that pretty much covers what you can expect at a weekly bracket race.

Suppose you've made five practice passes on the first day, recording the following times: 22.30; 21.11; 21.09; 21.10; 21.10. Other than that first run, which was your first of the weekend and should be discounted, the car has run a consistent 21.10. Your ET has been nice and consistent, and even though your RT, which has varied considerably and is not so predictable, the ET is a fairly certain thing.

So on your windshield you write your dial-in, which should be 21.10, with white shoe polish. At most tracks you simply have

to drive the car up to the staging area and the officials at the starting line will note the dial-in number and relay the information to the folks in the tower. At some places you may actually have to present the dial-in to an official. You'll have to determine the procedure for stating your dial-in at the track where you choose to run.

So here you are, staged next to a guy with a '55 Chevy with a big block. Although the '55 is faster, capable of mid-12's, the car's owner is new at this and doesn't want to install a roll cage so he runs it in Street class. And, even though the '55 is capable of running a 12.50, the guy goes with a safer 15.00 breakout time.

In terms of actual speed and time, the guy in the '55 is going to win. But remember that he has to do the same thing; he needs to predict what he's going to run for the next several passes as well. Although he posted relatively consistent times—15.10; 14.94; 15.06; 15.10; 15.04—he hasn't had a clean run.

He dials in at 15.05. Because of your high ET you will get a 6.05 second head start. Because his car is faster, he should catch you just at the finish line. Both of you stage, then

As you can probably guess by now, your dial-in strategy is largely dictated by who you are running against. When in staging, count backward to see who you will be paired up against. The person next to you 200 yards back in staging is not necessarily the one you will run against.

the Tree gives you your start ahead of him and, bang, you stomp on the accelerator, feeling like you've just cut the best light of the day.

You check the mirrors, and he is coming hard and fast and blows by you right at the line. After crossing the line, you slow down, make the turn at the end of the escape road and tuck in behind him as you idle back down the return road. Then you get the news at the time slip booth. You won because your opponent broke out, running a 13.97. You, on the other hand, hit your index dead on: 21.10, with a 0.670 reaction time. And, although you won that round and you're running consistently, you also got darned close to breaking out too. Although nothing about the car seems to have changed, it was a bit stronger. Perhaps this is due to change in track or weather conditions. At any rate, you're running awfully close to break out, so you might want to "dial down" a bit, perhaps to a 21.09 or a 21.08 just to be safe.

The next time you go to the staging lanes, walk back from the front, counting the cars to see who you will run against. You'll be running against a stock Mustang 5.0 with a dial-in of 14.29. You want to leave as quickly as possible this time to cut a better light than that last RT. And because it's not so new anymore, as the light flashes green you find yourself already on the way. You know you've cut a decent light.

The Mustang just got the start and you see it rock onto its back wheels, as it strains toward you. The Mustang is coming, gaining speed as you check the mirror again. So is the line. The Mustang is no longer in your rearview, but now looming large in your side mirror. You cross the line and he passes you just past the line.

You look at the wall just past the scoreboard and see that you got the win light. This time, after slowing down and taking the slip at the time slip booth, you find out that your ET was very close again. You did a 21.10 after dialing down. Then you look at the reaction time: 0.520, your best ever. The other guy ran a 14.31, with a 0.580 reaction time. You were tied on ET, that is you were both off by three hundredths of a second, but you beat him on reaction time—he was 6/100ths over package.

You're thinking victory banquet now. They call you again, and you roll up to the decreasing staging lane lines (we're in final eliminations now, remember?) and do the counting again, to determine who you'll be racing. The guy in your class is driving a beat-up Chevelle with a dial-in of 25.12. And you thought your LTD was embarrassing.

This time you line up, knowing the handicap is on his side. He goes first. Four seconds and some change goes by and you get your light. You throttle the car and are mildly concerned, figuring you blew the start a little, but you're still confident. You see him in the distance, and as you get close to the line, there he is, right beside you. You stomp the accelerator harder trying to squeeze some more out of the tug, but no dice. He screams past the light first, the little four-cylinder crying for mercy. You look at the wall. The win light is on his side. You broke out. A 21.07. Then you look at the RT: 0.831. You were caught trying to catch him at the line, thinking you were in a heads-up race without paying attention to the clock and your own dial in. A classic mistake, coupled with a very slow RT, which we'll address in a moment.

IMPROVING RT

Your RT probably needs some work, as does just about everyone else's. Although reaction time is somewhat dependent on inherent, natural ability, it can be exercised like any other body part and improved. Most beginners make the mistake of waiting for the green light to light before actually going. After all, this is what we are used to while waiting for a traffic light to change. But in drag racing, there is a slight delay between when the green light shines and when you trip the green. At the same time, it will take a good half to three-quarters of a second to make the car move once the green light comes on. Cutting a perfect light means you have to be that far ahead of the green light. You should be moving toward full acceleration as the final yellow is glowing.

When the light comes on, it takes time before you can actually move your left foot off the brake and some time before you plant your right foot on the gas. The time it takes is usually about a tenth to two-tenths of a second to actually move your foot to the full throttle position, and probably a few hundredths of a second to realize you can leave the line. Equally, there are a few fractions of a second from the time the lights flash and the time you register it in your brain. Instinctively, there are about two-tenths of a second that you have no control over. The time it takes for your car to move from a sta-

tic position to a moving start is also about one to two tenths. Bottom line, you can lose up to a half a second and still leave exactly on time. That's a career in drag racing—but it will be a short career, won't it?

After your first few rounds you'll be able to find out what your average RT is. If you're inconsistent, from .525 to .950, then practice is all you really need. But if you're always cutting a .950 or more each and every time, then you seriously need to evaluate your technique.

Practice

You can practice with a transbrake release or with a practice Christmas Tree, which is available from any number of drag racing magazines via mail order (see photo on page 102). Many racers find them beneficial, and some practice with them in the staging area.

Another method where you can really analyze what you're doing is to have a friend stand near the line in staging in such a way that he or she can frame the car and the Tree with a video camera (make sure it has a zoom). Have him tape the action whenever you come to the line.

View the tape when you get home (in fact,

This guy is doing more than just taking home movies. He's actually taping his friend's reaction time for slo-mo playback later.

"Figure out how fast your car responds, and note how quickly you can move once you get the cue, then work to improve your RT. If you're serious about this sport, invest in a practice timer— it will quickly pay for itself."

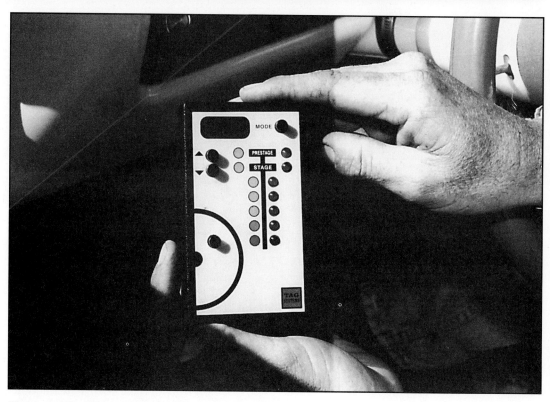

These practice Trees are great. They basically simulate the countdown, and start as though you are using a transbrake. You release the button when you start. Time is displayed in the upper left hand window. Short of endless real-life starts, this is the best practice you can get.

if you can, watch it right there at the track for instant instruction). Put the tape in and slow it down. You should be able to see exactly where you are failing. Watch the amber lights and how long it takes your car to move from amber to green. Most likely, you're just waiting too long to move to full throttle. You aren't slower, just more cautious. You don't want to red-light, so you play it safe.

So again, running the VCR in slow motion, watch the Tree. See how the lights seem to come on as if they have a rheostat, as if they are turned up and then down in intensity as if they are dining room lights with one of those dimmer switches?

But they don't. Light from artificial sources—especially lights with filaments (like Tree lights)—have to "power up." They don't just come on at full power. Start watching that. Look for the beginning of the glow to time your move to full throttle. That is one of the keys.

Another key is to take the view that the race doesn't start as the green comes on, it starts as the final yellow goes out (we're not talking about timing—that doesn't start until you move the car). Watch the video again. As the light dims slightly as it moves from yellow to green, you should be on your way at this point.

This is not an exact science. There are various stages to the Tree and various spans of time that it takes you to leave. It doesn't matter if you're extremely quick, if you wait too long to make the move as opposed to anticipating it correctly, you're still going to lose. Analyzing your responses and planning for them make all the difference in RTs. Figure out how fast your car responds, and note how quickly you can move once you get the cue, then work to improve your RT. If you're serious about this sport, invest in a practice timer—it will quickly pay for itself. ∎

BRACKET MATH

If you really want to get serious about bracket racing, then you'll need to take a serious approach. The purpose of this chapter is to help you take some of the guesswork out of setting up and running your car. By performing some very basic mathematical calculations, you can get a rough idea of such things as optimum shift points, estimating ET and MPH (without ever getting in the car!), determining the gearing effect of the oversize slicks you're going to run, and such things as the amount of weight transferred during acceleration. To perform the following calculations, you'll need to have access to scales capable of weighing your car. Moving companies usually allow public use of their scales for a small fee. There are also truck stations that

You can eliminate much of the guesswork involved in setting up your car, or predicting how it will run, by performing some basic math.

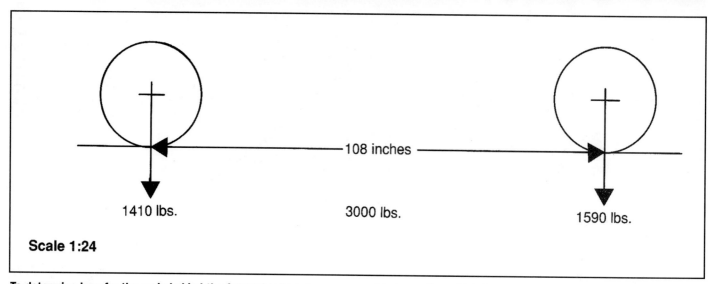

Scale 1:24

To determine how far the cg is behind the front wheel centers, you need to know the vehicle's rear wheel weight, overall weight and wheelbase.

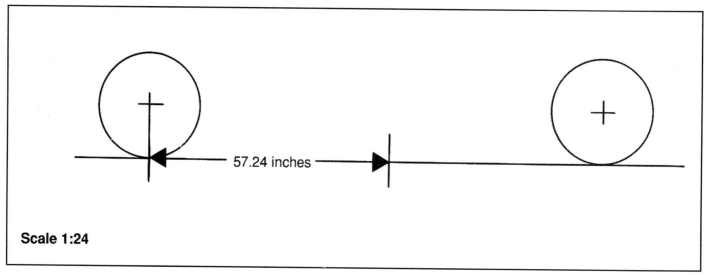

Scale 1:24

With weights of 1590 pounds on the rear wheels and 3000 pounds overall, and a wheelbase of 108 inches, the lengthways cg position would be 57.24 inches behind the front wheel centers.

have them as well. You will also need to have a good calculator, one capable of finding the cube root of a value.

CG LOCATION

The lengthways location of the center or gravity is measured as part of the wheelbase. To find how far it is behind the front wheel centers, divide the weight on the rear wheels by the overall vehicle weight and then multiply the resulting decimal figure by the wheelbase or:

cg Location = rear wheel weight/overall weight x wheelbase

As an example, suppose a car weighs 3,000 pounds overall, with 1410 pounds on the front wheels and 1590 pounds on the rear wheels. Now suppose the wheelbase is 108 inches (wheelbase can be found in a factory manual). Plugged into the formula:

cg Location = 1590/3000 x 108
cg Location = 0.53 x 108

You need to know the center of gravity of your car to help calculate the amount of weight transferred to the rear wheels, and to help with installing traction devices. The more weight you can transfer, the better the traction will be. Photo by Michael Lutfy.

The cg Location, lengthways, is located 57.24 inches behind the front wheel centers.

Sideways Location

The sideways location can be measured as part of the vehicle's track, which is the lateral distance between the centers of the treads of tires on either side. However, the sideways location of the cg is usually described in terms of how far it is off-center toward the heavier side. To find that, divide the weight on the lighter side by the overall weight and multiply the resulting decimal by the track, then subtract that figure from 1/2 the track or:

cg Location = track/2 - (weight on light side/overall weight x track)

If there is a significant difference between the front and rear tracks, use the average of the two.

cg Location = 63/2 - (1410/3000 x 63)
cg Location = 31.5 - (0.47 x 63)
cg Location = 1.89 inches

The sideways location of the center of gravity is 1.89 inches off-center on the heavy side to the left.

CG HEIGHT

One of the first things you need to figure out on your car is where its center of gravity (cg) is located. On an automobile with a front-mounted, pushrod V-8 engine and rear-wheel drive, which is the configuration of most traditional high-performance cars, the cg will usually be from 14 to 22 inches above the ground. To find the actual center of gravity, you must also determine the lengthways location, but for our bracket racing purposes, which is to ultimately calculate how much weight is transferred during acceleration, we only need to know the height.

On such a car as described above, one rule of thumb is that the cg will be at about the same height as the camshaft. To find what that height is, use a yardstick to measure from the ground to the camshaft centerline at the front of the engine. If all you are after

"On an automobile with a front-mounted, pushrod V-8 engine and rear-wheel drive, which is the configuration of most traditional high-performance cars, the cg will usually be from 14 to 22 inches above the ground."

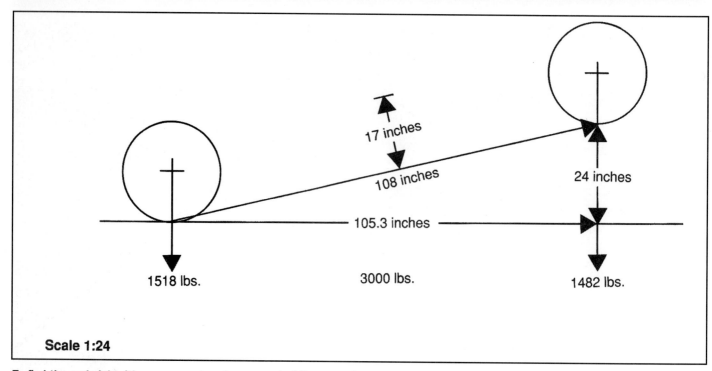

17 inches

108 inches

24 inches

105.3 inches

1518 lbs.   3000 lbs.   1482 lbs.

Scale 1:24

To find the cg height, it's necessary to raise one end of the car at least two feet, or 24 inches, as shown above, and record how much weight is added to the other end. The ground-level wheelbase must also be determined, either by measurement or geometric calculation. Applying the formula described in the text to the measurements in the drawing provides a cg height of approximately 17 inches.

are rough approximations, then skip the next few points, and jump right to the section on *Weight Transfer*. However, to pinpoint the cg height more precisely, or to find it at all on a vehicle with other than a front V-8 engine/rear-drive layout, you'll have to do some jacking around—literally.

Weights and Measures—Start again by weighing the vehicle at all four wheels. Although you can do it on the truck scale described at the beginning of this chapter, it will be a lot easier in this example if you could do it with a set of four scales. Record the overall weight and the front- and rear-wheel weights. Then raise one end—up to 24 inches if possible—with the wheels at the other end still on the scales, and note how much weight is transferred to that end. It doesn't matter which end of the vehicle is raised and which is left on the scales. Use a heavy-duty hydraulic jack or an overhead chain hoist to lift the vehicle. Don't even think about using a bumper jack. It wouldn't be likely to lift the vehicle high enough and,

as high as it did go, it wouldn't hold the vehicle safely while you take measurements underneath. At a truck scale, you would have to measure the overall weight, then drive the vehicle partway off the scale platform, jack up the end that's now clear and record the weight at the wheels still on the scale. That's a time-consuming activity not likely to endear one to the scale operator—or to any truckers waiting in line. You may, however, be able to go use the scales of a moving company, although they may charge you a small fee. With only two individual scales, you would have to weigh each end of the vehicle separately. At the opposite end, you would need two blocks the same height as the scales to place under the wheels to assure that the vehicle is level while being weighed. That would mean additional jacking as you swap the scales and blocks, stretching out what is already a tedious procedure. So, if at all possible, a set of four scales should be used.

Suspension and tire deflection could throw off your readings, so you should replace the shocks with metal rods of the same length, and tires can be overinflated to minimize deflection.

Suspension & Tire Deflection

At the end of the vehicle which remains on the scales, the added weight when the other end is raised could deflect the suspension and tires enough to throw off the readings. In addition, the suspension and tires at the raised end could drop slightly and prevent an accurate measurement of just how far that end has been lifted, a figure you'll need for calculating cg height. To deactivate the suspension at either end, the shock absorbers can be replaced with solid metal rods of the same length, while the tires on the scales can simply be overinflated to minimize deflection.

Full or Empty Fuel Tank

There are differences of opinion as to how much fuel should be aboard the vehicle while it is being weighed to find cg height. Some say that the tank should be full and others that it should be empty. Still others compromise by saying it should be half full—or half empty, depending on your point of view. One of the best suggestions

I've heard is to go through the whole procedure with the tank empty, then repeat it with the tank full. That will provide the two extremes in cg height that can occur in normal vehicle operation. Generally, on most conventional vehicles, the cg height is slightly lower with a full tank than it is with an empty one.

Necessary Dimensions

Once you know the weight of the vehicle and the amount of weight transferred when one end is raised, there are three dimensions in inches you need. The first is the wheelbase with the vehicle level, which you would most likely already know; the second is the wheelbase at ground level with one end raised; the third, as indicated earlier, is the distance that one end has been raised. The figures needed for the cg height on our example car are all shown in the drawing on the previous page. To find cg height, multiply the wheelbase with the vehicle level by the wheelbase with one end of the vehicle raised at least 24 inches by the added weight shown on the scales with the one end raised.

> *"Some say that the tank should be full and others that it should be empty. Still others compromise by saying it should be half full—or half empty, depending on your point of view. "*

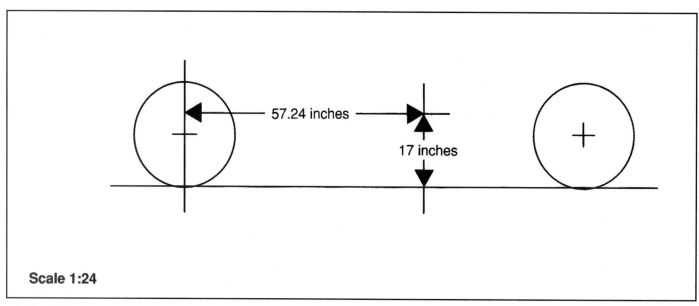

57.24 inches

17 inches

Scale 1:24

Now it's possible to graph the lengthways position, 57.24 inches behind the front wheels, and the vertical position, 17 inches. The sideways or lateral position can also be calculated easily, using the weight on the left or right wheels, the weight overall and the vehicle track.

Then divide the product of that calculation by the distance the one end has been raised multiplied by the overall vehicle weight. Or, stated as an equation:

cg Height = level wheelbase x raised wheelbase x added weight on scales / distance raised x overall weight.

As noted earlier, you would probably already know the level wheelbase of the vehicle and, of course, you could use a yardstick to check how high the one end has been raised.

Measuring Ground Level Wheelbase

To find the wheelbase at ground level with one end of the vehicle raised, you can either measure or calculate it. To measure it, drop a plumb bob from the bottom of one of the raised tires. Make a chalk mark where the plumb strikes the ground and, with a tape measure, find how far it is from the center of the ground level wheel on the same side of the vehicle.

Calculating Ground Level Wheelbase

To calculate the wheelbase at ground level, note in the figure that the two wheelbase measurements and the distance that one end of the vehicle has been raised form a right triangle. You would already know the measurements of two sides of that triangle—the 108-inch wheelbase with the vehicle level and the 24-inch distance that one end has been raised. You can find the third side by applying the Theorem of Pythagoras, which states that, in a right triangle, the square of the side opposite the right angle equals the sum of the squares of the other two sides.

The 108-inch wheelbase is the side opposite the right angle, and 108 squared is 11664. The other known side is the 24-inch lift, and 24 squared is 576. The square of the third side is 11664 minus 576, or 11088. The measurement of the third side would be the square root of 11088, or 105.3.

Added Weight—Finally, to find how much weight has been added on the scales, simply find the difference between the reading when the vehicle was level and the reading after the other end was raised. In our example, the first reading was 1410 pounds and the second 1518 pounds, a difference of 108 pounds. (It's simply coincidence in this case that the level wheelbase in inches and the added weight in pounds both happen to be 108.)

Calculating CG Height

Let's plug our figures into the formula and find the height of our bracket racer:

cg Height = 108 x 105.3 x 108/24 x 3000
= 1228219.2/72000

The answer is 17.0586, which of course can be rounded down to an even 17 inches, a typical figure for the type of car in question. In the figure nearby, the cg position both lengthways an vertically has been plotted.

WEIGHT TRANSFER

So why did we go through all of the trouble to find the height of our car's center of gravity? Mainly, so we can plug it into the formula to calculate how much of our car's weight is transferred to the rear wheels during acceleration. Weight transfer is critical because it can influence how a vehicle's chassis should be set up. But we are not there yet. There are still a few more values we have to determine first.

g Force

In order to find weight transfer during a particular maneuver, there are factors needed other than the position of the cg. One of the most important is the g (for gravity) force acting on the vehicle during the maneuver.

Here on earth, a free-falling object will gain speed every second by 32.174 feet per second or, as a physicist would say, it accelerates at 32.174 feet per second per second. That can also be written 32.174 feet per sec-

ond squared. That figure is 1.0 g and is the scientific norm for measuring the acceleration of any moving object, not just one in free fall. When you're in a rapidly accelerating vehicle and you feel as if you're being thrust back into your seat, you're experiencing g force. To find the g force acting on a car while it's accelerating, you need to know the thrust in pounds being applied by the drive wheels to the road surface. And to find the thrust at the drive wheels, you need to know the torque at the wheels and the rolling radius of the wheels and tires. Here, things begin to get a little complicated.

Drive Wheel Torque—To understand what is meant by drive wheel torque, you need to know that friction and inertia within the engine cause losses in horsepower and torque between the combustion chambers and the flywheel. Well, friction and inertia

The reason we went through all of that measuring and math work to find the cg height is because it is necessary in order to calculate the amount of weight transferred to the rear wheels. Photo by Michael Lutfy.

"To find the maximum torque in pounds-feet at the drive wheels, you have to multiply the torque at the flywheel by both the first-gear ratio and the final-drive ratio, and by our 0.85 efficiency factor."

By the time the power gets to the rear wheels, the drivetrain has siphoned off quite a bit. You can find out how much power has actually been consumed by placing the car on a chassis dyno. But if you don't have the money or access to one, you can figure that the loss is about 15% if the drivetrain is in good shape. So figure that the horsepower at the rear wheels is only 85% of the reported figure. If you have 100 horsepower at the flywheel, that means 85 horsepower. This number becomes a constant used in several equations.

also make some further claims between the flywheel and the drive wheels, with the transmission and final-drive assembly taking a particular toll on horsepower and torque. You can find the results of those losses by testing the vehicle on a chassis dynamometer, which measures output at the drive wheels. Or, you can simply estimate the losses at about 15 percent, which is what they're likely to be on most modern cars. In other words, the drivetrain should be about 85 percent efficient. A car which has 100 brake horsepower at the flywheel should have about 85 horsepower at the drive wheels. To find the maximum torque in pounds-feet at the drive wheels, you have to multiply the torque at the flywheel by both the first-gear ratio and the final-drive ratio, and by our 0.85 efficiency factor, or:

Drive Wheel Torque = flywheel torque x first gear ratio x final drive ratio x 0.85

Let's demonstrate that with an example, using a late-model Chevrolet Corvette with a 350-cubic-inch engine which has a maxi-

mum torque of 330 pounds-feet. The vehicle also has a 5-speed manual transmission with a 2.88:1 first gear and a 3.07:1 final-drive ratio. Applying those figures in the formula, you have:

Drive Wheel Torque = 330 x 2.88 x 3.07 x 0.85

That provides a figure of 2480.0688 or, rounded down, 2480 pounds-feet at the wheels. That's right—2480! No wonder it's easy to smoke a Corvette's rear tires in first gear!

Wheel Thrust—Torque can be described as a force in pounds applying leverage over a distance in feet; hence the definition of it in pounds-feet. At the drive wheels, that distance is determined by the tire size or, to be more precise, by the tire's rolling radius. That's the vertical measurement from the center of the wheel to the tire's point of contact on the ground. Because the weight of the vehicle flattens the tires slightly, the rolling radius is usually slightly less than the horizontal radius. To find the thrust in pounds the drive wheels apply to the pavement, divide the torque at the wheels in pounds-feet by the rolling radius in feet:

Wheel Thrust = drive wheel torque / rolling radius

Using a yardstick or tape measure, it's easier to get an accurate reading of the rolling radius in inches and convert it to feet, rather than trying to measure it directly in feet. On the Corvette, suppose the rolling radius is 12.6 inches. To convert that to feet, divide by 12, giving you a figure of 1.05 to divide into the drive wheel torque:

Wheel Thrust = 2480 / 1 .05

The thrust at the drive wheels is 2361.9048 or, rounded up, 2362 pounds.

Calculating g Force—Now we have all the info needed to calculate the g force during acceleration. To do so, you simply divide the thrust in pounds by the vehicle weight, or:

g Force = wheel thrust / weight

Given a weight of 3292 pounds for the Corvette, you would divide that into the thrust figure of 2362 pounds:

g Force = 2362 / 3292

The 'Vette's potential rate of acceleration would be 0.717497 or, rounded down, 0.72 g. We already know that 1.0 g equals 32.174 feet per second per second. Multiplying that by 0.72, the 'Vette's potential acceleration could also be expressed as 23.16528 or rounded off, 23 feet per second per second. Those are strictly theoretical figures, though, that don't take into account such variables as rolling resistance or aerodynamic drag. Nonetheless, if you know the maximum g forces for a variety of vehicles, they

do have comparative value.

Calculating Weight Transfer

Weight transfer is especially important in drag racing. As a car breaks from the line at the start of a 1/4-mile run, the weight that shifts momentarily to the rear will apply force to the drive wheels that should improve traction; the greater the weight transferred, the better the bite. To find a vehicle's maximum weight transfer during acceleration, multiply the overall weight by the height of the cg, divide that by the wheelbase, and then multiply the result by the g force, or:

Weight Transfer = weight x cg height / wheelbase x g

You already have a weight of 3292 pounds and a g force of 0.72 for the Corvette. Its cg height would be approximately 18 inches and its wheelbase 96.2 inches. So, to apply the formula:

Weight Transfer = 3292 x 18 / 96.2 x 0.72

The maximum potential weight transferred to the rear wheels during acceleration would be 443.49605 or, rounded down, 443 pounds. To show the effect of cg height on weight transfer, suppose you wanted to rebuild the Corvette for drag racing. You were able to jack it up enough that the cg was raised 6.0 inches to a height of 24 inches while, for the sake of simplicity, the other critical specs were kept the same:

Weight Transfer = 3292 x 24 / 96.2 x 0.72

That would increase weight transfer to 590.10124 or, rounded down, 590 pounds, a gain of over 33 percent or one-third! In actual practice, if the car were being prepared for the drags, the engine would have been modified for higher output and a

"Those are strictly theoretical figures, though, that don't take into account such variables as rolling resistance or aerodynamic drag. Nonetheless, if you know the maximum g forces for a variety of vehicles, they do have comparative value."

You can get an idea of what your car will do on the top end without leaving your living room.

numerically higher final-drive ratio installed. With greater torque and stronger gearing, the potential g force would have been raised and added still further to the amount of potential weight transfer. That explains why many drag cars, in classes which permit it, are built as high off the ground as they are.

CALCULATING ET AND MPH

If you can't wait to get to the drag strip and want a fairly rough idea of what your car will do, you can figure it out with a good calculator and the following formulas. You'll need to know the overall weight of the car and its horsepower. You can also figure out how much horsepower you'll need to go a certain ET, if you know the weight.

Elapsed Time

The formula for ET involves the cube root of the weight-to-power ratio multiplied by a constant of 5.825, while the formula for terminal mph calls for the cube root of the power-to-weight ratio multiplied by a con-

stant of 234. Note an important distinction here: For ET, you want weight-to-power, i.e., pounds per horsepower. For mph, you want power-to-weight, i.e., horsepower per pound.

$$ET = \sqrt[3]{Weight/hp} \times 5.825$$

Suppose you have a Corvette that weighs 3,440 pounds, complete with fuel and the driver aboard, with a 245-hp engine. If you plug those numbers into the formula above, its quarter-mile ET should be 14.05 seconds. *Road & Track* once tested just such a combination and posted an elapsed time of 14.6 seconds. Without considering any other variables, the formula has come within 4.0 percent of an actual test run.

Power or Weight from ET—From the formula for ET, formulas can be derived to find either power or weight, when the other is known. To find how much hp would be needed to propel a car of a given weight to a given ET, divide the weight by the cube of the ET divided by 5.825:

$$HP = \frac{weight}{(ET/5.825)^3}$$

For the 3440-pound 'Vette to post an ET of 14.05 seconds, it would need—surprise!—245 hp. If the unknown were the weight, you could find it with the cube of the ET divided by 5.825, multiplied by the hp:

$$Weight = (ET/5.825)^3 \times hp$$

And how much should the 245-hp, 14.05-second 'Vette weigh? The answer is 3438 pounds. (The calculator lost a couple of pounds in rounding errors.)

MPH

The formula for mph at the end of a quarter mile acceleration run is:

$$MPH = \sqrt[3]{hp/weight} \times 234$$

For the Corvette, the speed would be 97 mph. *Road & Track's* test figure was 95.5 mph. So, this time, the formula's error is less than 1.6 percent!

Power or Weight from MPH—Again, formulas can be derived to find either power or weight. To find the hp, the cube of the mph divided by 234 should be multiplied by the weight:

$$HP = (mph/234)^3 \times weight$$

To propel the 3440-pound 'Vette to 97 mph in the quarter mile, you'd need—yes—245 hp. To find the weight, the cube of 234 divided by the mph should be multiplied by the hp:

$$Weight = (234/mph)^3 \times hp.$$ Here, the weight works out to 3439.5 pounds, only 1/2 pound off.

Gearing for Quarter-Mile Speed

One of the tacit assumptions of these formulas is that the vehicle is properly geared and that, of course, may or may not be true. It's possible that the gearing might be too low—or too high—to enable the car to reach the quarter-mile speed indicated by the formula. However, once the potential speed has been calculated, there's a formula from

"It's possible that the gearing might be too low—or too high—to enable the car to reach the quarter-mile speed indicated by the formula."

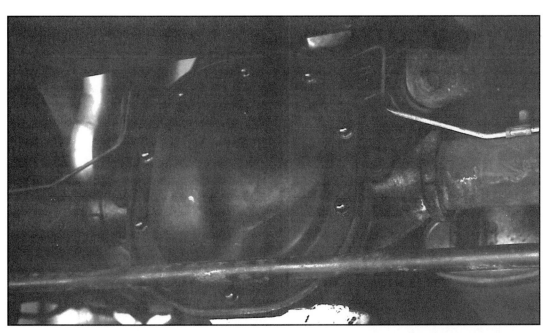

Before you tear apart the engine because the ET and MPH don't compute, check the gearing. Your car may not have the right ratio to reach the mph indicated by the formula. Photo by Michael Lutfy.

Shift indicators can tell you when to shift at a certain rpm. But the problem is, you need to tell it when to tell you to shift, so you'll need to have an idea of the optimum shift point for your car. Photo by Michael Lutfy.

How does that compare with the Corvette's actual gearing? Well, it has a 3.07 final drive but, as it cleared the end of the quarter, it was still in the 3rd of its 4 gears, with a ratio of 1.34. Multiplying 3.07 by 1.34, the overall ratio is 4:11. That's just slightly more than 4.0 percent off the formula's recommendation!

Auto Transmission

With an automatic transmission, the constant 335 replaces 340:

Overall Gear Ratio = tire diameter/335 x rpm/mph

Had the 'Vette been equipped with a Turbo Hydra-Matic, recommended overall gear ratio to reach a quarter-mile terminal speed of 97 mph would've been 4.3431297 or, rounded off, 4.34.

SHIFT POINTS

another source for determining the optimum overall gearing. It's from Larry Shepard of Mopar Performance and, for a car with a manual gearbox, it is:

Overall Gear Ratio = Tire Diameter/340 x rpm/mph

The Corvette discussed earlier has 275/40ZR17 tires, which would have a diameter of 25.66 inches. (How we found the diameter is explained next.) The engine could be revved easily to 5500 rpm and the formula predicted a speed at the end of the quarter mile of 97 mph. Plugging the necessary figures into Shepard's formula:

Overall Gear Ratio = 25.66/340 x 5500/97

Overall Gear Ratio = 0.0754706 x 56.7

The recommended overall gear ratio would be 4.279183, or about 4.28.

Some of the electronic goodies we've talked about require you to program shift points based on engine rpm. To get the best acceleration out of a high-performance vehicle during shifts, hot rodders say you should stay "on the cam." What they mean is that you should keep the engine within an rpm range where the transmission is delivering optimum torque before and after each shift. The first step toward finding what that range might be is to use a dyno chart, like the one shown on page for a typical 350 cid Chevy engine. In order to calculate shift points, though, you'll be primarily concerned with rpm and torque, not horsepower, because it's torque that accelerates an automobile. Next, you need to know the loss or gain in rpm when you shift from one gear to another.

Example—Suppose you have a Chevrolet powered by the modified 350 cubic-inch engine with output specifications shown in the dyno chart, with a Warner T-10 4-speed gearbox which has ratios of 2.20 in 1st, 1.66

DYNO CHART

RPM	LB-FT	BHP
3000	340	194
3200	340	207
3400	345	223
3600	345	236
3800	350	253
4000	350	267
4200	340	272
4400	335	281
4600	330	289
4800	325	297
5000	315	300
5200	310	307
5400	305	314
5600	305	325
5800	305	337
6000	300	343
6200	280	331
6400	255	311
6600	240	302
6800	190	246
7000	160	213

These output figures are based on a typical 350 Chevrolet with mild modifications. Use them to help you calculate the formulas for shift points.

RPM After Shift = 1.66/2.20 x 6000
 = 0.7545455 x 6000
 = 4527 rpm

The engine speed in 2nd will be 4527 rpm. Subtracting that figure from 6000, you'll find you have a drop of 1473 rpm or about 25 percent. Obviously, you can also apply the formula to shifts from 2nd to 3rd and from 3rd to 4th. From 2nd to 3rd, the engine speed will drop from 6000 to 4735 rpm, a loss of 1265 rpm or 21 percent; from 3rd to 4th, it will fall from 6000 to 4580 rpm, losing 1420 rpm or 27 percent.

Driveshaft Torque

But, given the torque characteristics shown on the dyno chart, is 6000 rpm the best point at which to upshift? To answer that question, you need to know the driveshaft torque being delivered to the rear wheels before and after each shift. That's simply a matter of multiplying the brake torque at the flywheel by the transmission ratio, or:

Driveshaft Torque = flywheel torque x transmission ratio

According to the dyno chart, you have 300 pounds-feet of torque at the flywheel at 6000 rpm. With a 1st gear ratio of 2.20, that becomes 660 pounds-feet being delivered from the transmission via the driveshaft to the drive wheels. Won't the output from the transmission to the driveshaft be slightly less than the input to the transmission from the flywheel? Yes, it will be. But it doesn't really affect the comparative validity of our driveshaft torque figures so, to simplify your calculations, you needn't take it into account here.

All right, you have 660 pounds-feet of driveshaft torque at 6000 rpm in 1st gear. When you shift into 2nd, the rpm drops to 4527. According to the dyno chart, the engine has 330 pounds-feet of torque at

"But, given the torque characteristics shown on the dyno chart, is 6000 rpm the best point at which to upshift? To answer that question, you need to know the driveshaft torque being delivered to the rear wheels before and after each shift."

in 2nd, 1.31 in 3rd and direct 1.00 drive in 4th. When you drag race, you shift at 6000 rpm. How much rpm do you lose during the shift from, say, 1st to 2nd? You can find out by dividing the ratio in 1st gear into the ratio in 2nd. The result will be a percentage which, when multiplied by the rpm in 1st, will provide the equivalent rpm in 2nd. Or, expressed as an equation:

RPM After Shift = ratio shift into/ratio shift from x rpm before shift

With the Warner T-10, divide the 2.20 1st-gear ratio into the 1.66 2nd-gear ratio and multiply by 6000:

Before you go bolting on bigger tires, you should first estimate the effect they will have on your drive ratio. Photo by Michael Lutfy.

4600 rpm. Multiply that by a 2nd gear ratio of 1.66 and the result would be 548 pounds-feet of driveshaft torque. During the shift from 1st to 2nd, you've lost 112 pounds-feet of driveshaft torque or about 17 percent. A 17-percent drop in torque during an upshift doesn't sound like a good way to win a drag race.

EFFECT OF OVERSIZE TIRES

As mentioned in the chapter on suspensions, you may want to add some bigger Mickey Thompson or McCreary street/strip tires, or bigger drag slicks. But if you bolt on larger tires, your ET may change considerably, and you'll be running around trying to determine why. Fortunately, if you know the diameters of both the new and old tires and the vehicle's existing final-drive ratio, you can calculate the effects the bigger tires will have ahead of time. The source where you purchased the tires should have the diameter of the tire you are running. Or you can simply apply a tape measure to one of the tires currently on your car and to one of those you're considering as replacements.

Section Height & Width

You may also be able to figure out the diameters of the tires based on their respective sizes. In the old days when 6.00x16 was the standard size on many popular cars, that was easy. The tire's section height—the distance between the edge of the rim and the face of the tread—and the section width—the distance between the sidewalls on either side—were about the same. In the case of a 6.00x16, the section height and width were both about 6.0 inches and the tire was mounted on a 16-inch wheel. To find the diameter, you simply multiplied the section height, 6.0 inches, by 2, giving you 12 inches, and added that to the wheel rim diameter, 16 inches, for an overall figure of 28 inches.

Aspect Ratio

Modern passenger car tires and light duty truck tires aren't sized quite so simply. In most cases, their section height and width are no longer alike. The height is usually much less than the width, and the relationship between the two—the aspect ratio—is an important part of their specs. The aspect ratio is the percentage the section height is of the section width. Generally, passenger car and light truck tires are now produced in metric sizes that indicate the section width in millimeters, the aspect ratio in percent and the wheel rim diameter in inches.

As a case in point, let's take a P235/75R15 tire. The "P" means it's a passenger tire; if it were a light truck unit, it would have the initials "LT" instead. Similarly, the "R" means it's a radial, while a "B" would indicate it's bias belted. The "235" is the section width in millimeters and the "75" is the aspect ratio, indicating that the section height is 75 percent of the section width. Finally, the "15" is the rim diameter in inches.

Metric Diameter—To find the diameter in inches of a metric size tire, you must first find the section height in inches. To do that, you convert the section width, 235 millimeters in our example, to inches by dividing it by 25.4, the number of millimeters in an inch. Then you convert the aspect ratio, 75, to a decimal figure by dividing it by 100. Multiply the quotients of these two calculations together to find the section height in inches. Double that figure and add the wheel rim diameter, which is already given in inches, and the result will be the diameter of the tire in inches. Expressed as a formula, that would be:

2 x section width/25.4 x aspect ratio/100 + rim dia.

That can be simplified somewhat to:

Tire Diameter = 2 x section width x aspect ratio/2540 + rim dia.

Plug in the appropriate specs for a P235/75R15 tire:

Tire Diameter = 2 x 235 x 75/2540 + 15
Tire Diameter = 2 x 6.9 + 15

That would work out to a section height of 6.9 inches and an overall diameter of 28.88 inches which, of course, could be rounded

up to 28.9 inches.

Effective Drive Ratio

To find what the effective overall drive ratio would be with a given increase in tire diameter, the formula is:

Effective Ratio = Old tire dia./new tire dia. x original ratio

Example—Suppose you have a set of 28.9-inch P235/75RlSs on a Camaro with a 3.08 final-drive ratio and you want to replace them with 33-inch 33x12.50xl5s. To find the effective drive ratio with the bigger tires, the figures would be:

Effective Ratio = 28.9/33 x 3.08
Effective Ratio = 0.8757576 x 3.08

With the bigger tires, the effective ratio is only 2.70! That's enough of a change to cause a noticeable loss in responsiveness.

Equivalent Drive Ratio

To find the final-drive ratio needed with the new tires to provide the equivalent of the vehicle's performance with the original tires, the formula is:

Equivalent Ratio = new tire diameter/old tire diameter x original ratio

Note that the positions of the tire diameters in this formula are reversed from their positions in the formula for effective ratio. In the case of the switch from 28.9- to 33 inch tires on a vehicle with a 3.08 final drive, the figures would be:

Equivalent Ratio = 33/28.9 x 3.08

Equivalent Ratio = 1.1418685 x 3.08

That works out to 3.51, so a set of final-drive gears in the 3.50-plus range would be needed to restore the lost responsiveness. ■

"But if you bolt on larger tires, your ET may change considerably, and you'll be running around trying to determine why."

The faster you go, the more safety equipment you'll need in order to pass tech to race. Photo by Michael Lutfy.

Some things must be assumed as truth, regardless of whether you believe them to be or not: First; you should be concerned for your safety. Second, if you are not concerned, the NHRA is concerned for you and about your participation in their sport.

GENERAL SAFETY

The NHRA, or whatever sanctioning body happens to be supervising or sanctioning your racing series, is not vindictive, but if you insist on endangering other competitors and the reputation of a sport which has been taken from outlaw to front row, you'll be ousted.

All sanctioning bodies with any credibility will not allow you to compete with a vehicle which is not up to safety specs. Each class has different levels of safety requirements. Pick up a current rulebook for the sanctioning body you'll be running with. For the most part, tracks will be either sanctioned by or will be utilizing NHRA rules (tracks which are not running weekly

Although slower classes do not require one, it is always advisable to wear a Snell-approved racing helmet. You never know what can go wrong. You are still running your car at its maximum in a manner is was not built for.

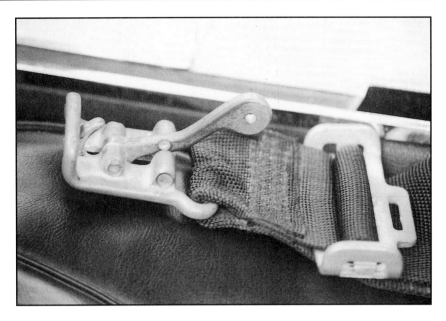

Stock seat belts just don't cut it. You should install racing belts, with strong webbing and quick release mechanisms, if your speeds are higher than 100 mph.

NHRA programs are often insured by the NHRA and thus strictly follow NHRA regulations for both track and participant guidelines). For most classes, you need to have nothing but a safe and sound car. What that means is that all components should be securely fastened to the car. This doesn't mean that an axle which is tied to the frame by good strong climber's rope is going to be considered safe. Neither is a hood taped on with duct tape.

Street and Sportsman

For the basic classes, which include Street and Sportsman you need the following: Your car must have seat belts, which should be bolted to the floor or frame. Seat belts are good things—even if they do keep you in the car as the accident is happening when you would rather be somewhere else.

You need a 16-ounce coolant overflow can which should empty off the radiator. The battery may remain in the stock location, but the tie-downs must be in good condition and should keep the battery stable. There's nothing like a fifty pound projectile roaming the engine compartment at 95mph. If you decide to move the battery, you can no longer use J-bolts, even if they were OEM before you went crazy with the wrenches and wire cutters. If you did move the battery, you'll need an emergency shut off at the rear of the vehicle (depending on the class of car, you may have needed that anyway). In any event, battery systems must be separated from the driver's area by a metal bulkhead, so you can't just bolt the battery to the floor behind your seat.

The firewall must be free of holes and all interior paneling that is not stock must be at least .032 inch aluminum or .024 inch steel (no magnesium, since it can burn). The driver's side door panel must be covered. The ignition switch must be accessible to the driver, and it must be self-starting, which in the best of times can sometimes be a problem.

All fuel tanks must be externally vented and no higher than the top of the rear tire. Fuel regulators must be six inches forward of the bellhousing and/or firewall. Rubber fuel line is restricted to 12 inches maximum from front to rear. Gas caps are mandatory. And all carburetors must be covered with something resembling an air cleaner. By the way, if you want a way-cool hoodscoop, it must not be higher than 11 inches above hood level.

The tires must be considered safe and must have 1/16th inch of tread and be free of

Roll cages are added insurance. Bolt-in cages allow you to install one without heavy welding or tearing up your interior.

nails and such, which makes perfect sense. And hub caps and trim rings must be removed.

Nitrous oxide, if mounted in the driver's compartment, must be equipped with relief valve and vented outside of the driver's compartment. No need to be laughing uncontrollably on the starting line. And you can't have nitrous on supercharged engines, because that's like sitting on a time bomb.

No loose or liquid ballast (weight) allowed. All ballast must be installed with 2 1/2-inch diameter bolts.

All windows must be clear, with factory tinting the exception. No flexible exhaust pipe is allowed, and exhaust must be routed away from the driver and the fuel tank. In addition, you can't have plastic oil lines in the driver's compartment, nor should you have any loose instrumentation, or equipment in the cockpit. Take out the CDs, put the spare change in your pockets and leave the fuzzy dice in the pits with your lunch.

Traction bars and mounting brackets can-

not be lower than the lowest edge of the wheel rim, and if not attached at the front you need a U-bolt or a strap.

Non-stock automatic floor-mounted shifters must be equipped with a positive reverse lock-out which should be secured to the shifter and not the frame. They don't want you going backward during staging. A functional neutral safety switch is mandatory.

11-14 Second Cars

Flywheel and clutch must meet SFI Spec or 1-1 or 1-2 and flywheel shield meeting SFI spec 6-1 or 6-2 mandatory in any car running 11.99 or under with manual transmission, which means if you don't know what it is, you probably aren't legal—or you aren't in this class.

The car must have a minimum of three inches of ground clearance and it must have shock absorbers. It should have no fluid leaks—which may be a huge problem for some of you—and should be neat and clean so the tech inspector can look at it and see, say, the oil pan through all the sludge. Good news: you only need one working taillight.

No naked racing: you need a shirt and full-length pants while in competition. No tank tops, bare torsos or exposed feet. This is racing, after all.

For cars which can travel the 1,320 at 13.99 seconds or quicker, you must have a helmet that meets Spec 31.2 or Snell 80, 85, or 90 codes.

All convertibles running 12.00 to 13.99 seconds must have an approved roll bar and head protector sufficiently padded and utilize an approved five point quick release seat belt shoulder harness (SFI Spec 16.1) with three-inch-wide straps inspected or replaced at two-year intervals plus face shields or goggles.

Under 11 Seconds

If your car runs 10.99 or quicker you need heavy-duty aftermarket axles. All cars must

Even if you opt for a fully welded cage, you can install one of these swing-out bars to help get in and out.

have approved roll bar, side bar and head protector (padded) and utilize a five point safety harness (SFI Spec 16.1) with three inch wide straps inspected or replaced at two-year intervals.

As an aside, roll cages are not a bad idea even if your car runs in the 20s, but more interestingly—and following the latest trend—many people are using their cars as dual purpose racers. If you have something like a late-model Ford Mustang or a Camaro—something nimble on a road course but equipped with plenty of power—you can put a roll cage in it for the purpose of drag racing, but then can use it in either SCCA Solo II or even showroom stock racing. Since in either class a bolt-in cage is acceptable, some competitors are choosing to do both, simply changing and adjusting the car to adapt it to either type of racing. If this appeals to you you might consider a cage which will fit each. Make sure you don't make a mistake when you make the purchase.

You'll need an aftermarket harmonic balancer, which is mandatory on all cars running 10.99 seconds or quicker (SFI Spec 18.1), and your manual transmission requires an explosion proof flywheel, clutch, pressure plate and flywheel shield meeting SFI Spec 1-1, or 1-2.

Should you be rich or lucky enough to have a car which runs in the nines or below, you not only need a NHRA or equivalent

license, but also a FAA physical (from the Federal Aviation Administration, which certifies pilots ... and figuring on the Gs that a serious dragster puts you through, that is an appropriate entity to be doing these things).

All drivers in the faster classes must comply with NHRA or IHRA clothing specifications, with neck collar, a crotch strap, and all cars must have approved roll cages with sidebar and driver's ribbon type window net permanently secured at the bottom. NHRA or IHRA clothing specs are basically that you must wear a protective jacket, arm restraints and gloves in open-bodied cars running 11.99 seconds or quicker. In addition, a master cut-off switch with on-off clearly marked is required And if you car is really flyin', a parachute is required with top speeds of 150 mph or more.

Be Responsible for Your Own Safety

Safety equipment is perishable. The webbing in your belts has a life span. Most people feel the belts are useless after one season. That may not be completely accurate but at the same time leaving the car with the same belts you bought back when Nixon was president is not exactly safe strategy. They become brittle and will break under stress. If you use your head for a second you'll realize that the only time they'll really be under stress is when you need them in a rollover. Don't wait forever to change them.

"As an aside, roll cages are not a bad idea even if your car runs in the 20s, but more interestingly— and following the latest trend— many people are using their cars as dual purpose racers."

Being responsible for your own safety means installing items that may not be required for your class, but are a good idea anyway. This is a driveshaft hoop, designed to prevent the driveshaft from "windmilling" up through the floorboards if it should break. Photo by Michael Lutfy.

In addition, you must do your own due diligence, meaning the tech inspectors, as good as they are, may miss safety problems on your car. Check your own tires. Make sure they are free of debris like tacks and so forth and have no cuts or potential puncture spots (like places that have been pinched against the rim). Make sure the lugs are tight, the motor mounts are sound and the axles are secure.

Also remember that there are other days of racing; if you're racing your street car, there are days you'll need to use the car—like to get home, for instance. Don't blow it up or ball it up. Make sure the car has plenty of clean oil, the coolant system is full and in proper order and if there is a problem, don't continue. Go home and fix it. Better to lose $20 in entry fees that $2,000 in engine repairs.

CAR CONTROL

Speaking of good judgment and knowing when to call it quits, it might be appropriate at this point to discuss car control. Car control is far more a safety issue than a performance issue. Drag racing tends to be pretty straightforward in terms of car control, pun intended. You point the car in the right direc-

tion as you get to the starting line and, hopefully, you don't have to move the wheel much until it's time to make the turn onto the return road.

But there's a lot that happens after you just floor the car. Not only do you have to keep it straight during acceleration, but you are also busy making sure you don't overrev, you may be shifting gears, and you may have to keep an eye on your mirror or on the clock and adjust your speed to avoid breaking out. There's a lot of room for error. Furthermore, there's always the possibility that something mechanical will go wrong— a cut tire, blown engine, or the other guy losing control and crossing into your lane.

Planting your foot in an underpowered car and not getting out of the throttle until after you've passed the finish line is a relatively easy task. That's why there is a High School division. Unless the car is capable of 10s, it shouldn't be much of a handful—unless the driver decides he's about to break out.

Sometime a few years back in Northern California, a pair of Corvettes were running together on the 1320, with one car heavily modified and the other stock. The difference in dial-in was a few seconds. The stock 'Vette moved out first when the Tree changed, and three or four seconds later the faster car got the green. The stock car was a dot on the horizon, but because of all the trick stuff on the modified car, the faster car quickly caught and passed the stock 'Vette. Realizing he was about to break out, the faster car didn't just let off the accelerator, but literally stomped on the brakes. Smoke came off the tires, the car got sideways, and the slower car rammed into it. Both cars rolled over, (only one had a cage) and both were totalled.

The racer in the modified car did not take into account how fast his car could react when he stomped on the brakes. All he cared about was not breaking out. This is a classic racing mistake made by inexperienced racers.

In racing, you must be aware of what's going on around you at all times, and your senses should be tuned to what the car is doing. Your actions should be deliberate. True, you have to think fast and react accordingly, but you must also control your environment, and you can't do that if you are speeding along, a passenger in your own car.

You have essentially one job, which is to keep the car straight. The second job is to actually get it slowed down after the race is over. You may need to adjust your speed accordingly just before the end of the strip, but by degrees, not abruptly.

So what can happen to get the car off its course?

Let's discuss a few possibilities in order of importance. The majority of the problems you'll have will be in the first 220 feet. Most of the time, the problem here is a result of a loss of traction. Assuming you have limited slip in the rear end, and there's no traction, and you're at full tilt, the car will tend to rotate to one side or the other. One wheel will gain adhesion more than the other, or worse still, one wheel will stop spinning and grab the pavement.

Although you may think that you can save the car from spinning, your first lesson should be that if there is a sign of trouble, get out of it immediately. No race is worth the risk of hurting yourself or someone else.

Frank Hawley, of The Drag Racing School in Gainesville, Florida, and Pomona, California, doesn't even teach evasive car control in any of his classes. Says Hawley: "What we spend our time doing is teaching (students) how *not* to get sideways. We don't even touch on accident avoidance, because if the car gets sideways they've already made a mistake. The intent of our program has always been to get people to understand what's going on; to know how the car should be doing, how the car should be feeling, how they should be responding to what the car's doing down the race course and how to avoid ever getting in trouble. Most of the accidents you see in racing are avoidable from the driver's seat before they happen."

Then Hawley said succinctly: "If the car wiggles, you close the throttle and stop the run. There's no use trying to teach a driver how to drive the car on a slippery race track. If it's that bad, you simply don't drive the car. That's how you avoid getting in trouble. If you spend the time telling people, 'Well, if you get sideways this is what you do...', you make that an option. It's not an option. Don't ever get into that situation."

So that's how you control the car. You

Whether it's in the burnout box or at mid-track, if the car starts to get sideways, the best thing to do is step out of the throttle imme-diatley. Don't be a hero trying to save it.

If something does go wrong on the top end, get the car slowed down as gently as possible. Apply even, moderate brake pressure, and don't jerk the wheel. You are traveling at a high rate of speed, and a sudden pitch will upset the car's balance. In this picture, the car on the left blew a motor, but the driver didn't panic. He slowed the car down gently, using all of the available runout.

don't. After a few years of experience, you can begin to use your judgment. Perhaps some problems are not as severe in consequences as others, but that will take a lot of time to develop. For the mean time, use discretion and abort the run.

Braking

Braking, on the other hand, needs to be carried out with very smooth movements. Don't stomp the pedals—especially at or near the finish line. Ease off the throttle, and ease on the brake. Once the weight has begun transferring and the car has a forward attitude, then do your heavy braking. But never slam on the brakes to slow down, fearing you'll break out. Think ahead. You'll have another chance next week. If you crash your car—or hurt yourself or others—you won't be back to compete in it. Be alert and save your car—as well as yourself—for another day.

All of this is very important stuff. Not only in theory, but in practice too. What that means is that safety and how you address it is like the credit report for officials. In other words, if you are a neophyte, this will be your first exposure to the politics of drag racing. You want to be remembered as a jerk? Show up with an unsafe car, drive badly and then, when an official mentions something to you, start an argument. They will never, ever forget you. That's not a good thing.

If you comply and have a little humility, you'll be surprised at what it will get you next time. You'll eventually get a reputation for being a good competitor and then, when you really need a break, they'll be far more liable to give it to you.

But for the time being remember that you're reading this book because you want some help. The tech inspectors are an extension of everything that is good about the sport of drag racing. If you regard them as the enemy you have missed the point of this sport and why it has become as popular as it has. Really, truly, they are trying to help you, not keep you off the track. Please listen to them, do what they say, and treat them with some courtesy. ■

BEYOND BRACKETS

12

Depending on where you're headed with bracket drag racing, after a few races you'll have established either a new potential career or a good hobby.

As a bracket drag racer, you can devote as much time and money as you choose in this sport without any worries about either going too far, or in fact, doing too much. If you wish to do more, go faster, make changes, be more innovative, take chances, spend money and be the king of your local race track, nobody will try to stop you as long as you put no one—including yourself—in danger.

By the same token, if you decide that you want to go back to college and can only afford to drive a beater—but still wish to participate—nobody will say a thing about that either.

Somewhere between these two extremes you will probably fall; not so poor that you

Do you have what it takes to move up to the pros? It's a long, hard road, one that few travel successfully. Be sure you master the bracket level before you even think about moving up.

Having a world champion driver certainly helps, but it is no guarantee of success. Scott Kalitta has paid his dues and proven himself more than once. He's currently a two-time Top Fuel Champion, and actively seeking his third title.

can't afford to do some modifications, but not so rich that you're going to gold plate your nitrous fittings.

But what if you discover, to your own surprise, that you have "the gift?" What if you can cut a perfect light every time? What if you can tune your car perfectly to nail the index each and every time, no matter what the track conditions are?

MOVING UP

Like anything else in your life, you have to take racing in stages. There is a definite learning curve to the process, no matter how talented you are. It is extremely rare that you can go out and run Top Fuel after just a few brackets, or even right from the beginning (it is also not advisable, for obvious safety reasons). You have to pay some dues and start at the bottom, which is where you are at now—bracket racing. Before moving up, you must master this level. Concentrate on improving yourself more than your car, and always be open-minded. Confidence will come from knowledge. The more open-minded you can be the more you will absorb. But if you are quick, if you can translate the buzzes and groans and can read the weather and adjust that fuel mix each

and every time you run the car, then take it to the next step.

"The sport can be real good to you and it can be real bad for you," veteran NHRA pro driver Al Hoffmann said. "Every year, every week, my parents and friends told me to get a job. I used to hear it all the time.

"I won the first drag race I ever entered. It was at Dover Dragstrip at Wingdale, New York, in 1968. That was the first (year). Then the following year I won 27 races. Now its tougher. You get a hundred cars in the class and it gets difficult. You'd run for your class and a trophy and then you'd run for cash.

"I just started it as a hobby. It's a good way for people to get started now. You gotta start somewhere. After doing it for nearly ten years I decided to make a living at it. I had a construction business and sold it and bought a Funny Car operation in 1970, and I've been doing it ever since."

Racing National Events

So to paraphrase Hoffmann: don't move up before you have completed the learning curve. In other words, move from Street to Pro by changing cars. First do the minimum adjustments and modifications to get the feel of the next level. Don't take the usual step of throwing money at it to do better. Once you're in that upper class, get an idea of how it works, keep your eyes open, learn from this new group of people. The more professional the class, the more experienced the racers tend to be, and the more you will learn.

From Pro, move up and perhaps into Divisional racing. Once you do three Divisionals you can run a National event, meaning you can run with the big boys when they come to town. You'll be able to work and walk down in the pits with the best in the business. Again, keep your eyes open and keep improving. Eventually, you might decide to get into an alcohol dragster or something like that.

"But if you are quick, if you can translate the buzzes and groans and can read the weather and adjust that fuel mix each and every time you run the car, then take it to the next step."

Here's the ultimate goal; a ride with a pro Top Fuel team backed by a major sponsor. McDonald's is now a major sponsor of the NHRA circuit. Getting to this point is by no means impossible, but it sure isn't easy.

Racing Schools

On the other hand, don't assume everything will always go smoothly. You may plateau and not get any farther in your own performance. Don't give up. Instead, consider enrolling in a driving school that emphasizes drag racing. The instructor of a good high performance drag racing school will give you a better idea of what's happening inside your race car and will tell you why it happens and what to do when it does. There are little things you may never have thought about; things you may never have considered important which will be explored thoroughly in school.

Probably the two best schools in the country are Roy Hill's Drag Racing school in Rockingham, North Carolina, and The Drag Racing School run by Frank Hawley in Gainesville, Florida. Both will accept either true neophytes or experienced pros and have shown consistent results with each group.

"There are little things you may never have thought about; things you may never have considered important which will be explored thoroughly in school."

After you master brackets, the next logical step up would be to a Super Comp or Gas class. Photo by Michael Lutfy.

They teach preparation, both physical and mental, and help you develop a regimen to follow each and every time you get behind the wheel to race.

Students discover what happens in a race car at speed. They learn about control, physical dynamics, and mostly about speed and power that is drag racing. In Hawley's Alcohol Dragster course one of the goals for new students is to simply be able to keep the throttle all the way down during a pass. You do that, they say, and you're on your way.

Each school offers many different categories of cars, but the major courses deal with Super Comp and Super Gas cars plus Pro Stock and Dragster instruction. Roy Hill is known for his Pro Stock Class and Hawley for his Alcohol Dragster course, but both give good instruction in the basics of drag racing. By the time you read this there may be more qualified schools, and as we said, these are not the only two now in existence, but they are very good.

Both tend to focus on reaction time as the key in drag racing and two ways to improve it is in focus and accurate anticipation. "One of the keys in drag racing is in concentra-tion," Hill said. "Say you've been out racing three to five years, you've had some success and you want to take it to a higher level. We'll help you. Or say you've never done it. If I have someone who's never done it, it's easier to teach them the right way to start. If a person has done it for a number of years they've got some bad habits. So we take them and give them a push in the right direction."

Frank Hawley explained, "We've spent time with drivers who've won more national events than I ever won and we work with them at a very sophisticated level. We work with them on sports psychology. We have some very advanced equipment to train with in terms of timing. By the same token, we are also equipped to take someone who's never seen a drag race to try it out in a very safe environment and experience it.

"Most of what we do now is with bracket racing (drivers). We use our cars but we also offer reaction time clinics around the country where you can bring your own cars. We specifically work on reaction times. It's a one-day program about three and a half to four hours of classroom seminar and then we put this special equipment on the cars which separates the driver reaction time from the car's reaction time. And then they get to do some on track testing to find out some things that they've never been able to find before. It's a really comprehensive program. The situation is, that the better the person is, the more they're going to get out of the program."

At this writing, Hill's three-day course offers a choice of Super Gas, Super Comp and Bracket Racing, or you can have training in Pro Stock and Pro Modified. They also work with people with alcohol cars and Top Fuel cars, and have courses specializing in acceleration and deceleration only.

"We teach people how to have mental and physical control, of themselves. When you reach that point where you have mental and physical control you'll feel it. You'll know how to win races," Hill said. "I've worked with sports psychiatrists and we deal with all forms of sports. We spend two hours in the classroom roughly. From there on out, the race car is the classroom. We video every move that you make—we have in-car cameras. We evaluate each run and you get started."

Some of what the schools teach has little or nothing to do with drag racing per se, but is of paramount importance in drag racing. Confidence and control are goals instructors strive to instill in their students. Without both confidence and control, they feel, you can't win; at least not consistently.

Hawley added, "If you're already a pro driver you probably already have some of that skill. I'm not teaching them how to drive the car. I'm teaching them how to focus better, teaching mental, visual development, and some technical aspects of human physiology and reaction time and those sorts of things. I'm not telling him how to drive the car. He's already there."

The secrets of learning to race well are difficult to share in a few points, but you should call the driving schools and make a choice as to where you want to go. These cars look a lot slower than they really are and before you spend a dime you need to know that this is something you really want to do.

The next step is, once you've found out you like it, sit down and determine your budget. Talk to a few local racers and find out how much it takes to run a competitive

> *"We teach people how to have mental and physical control of themselves. When you reach that point where you have mental and physical control, you'll feel it. You'll know how to win races."*

Kenny Bernstein is a businessman first and a racer second. When just starting out, he drove amateur classes for a while, then once he decided he wanted to take it seriously, he went back to business, building it up enough to allow him to return to racing with good cars to be competitive enough to attract major sponsorship. Photo by Michael Lutfy.

Joe Amato is another example of someone who raced since he was a kid, but became a successful businessman first in order to pursue a racing career. He's the owner of Keystone Automotive, a large wholesale auto parts distributor, but also one of the winningest Top Fuel drivers in the sport.

car. There's a lot more to it than you think. Just because you see an ad in the paper for a car for $25,000 doesn't mean that's all it will cost to go racing. You'll need the truck or a trailer and the tools or the garage to keep it in. That's before you even fire it up. You need to budget for everything.

The third thing is to be very patient about how quickly you're going to succeed at this. You've got to understand that this is something you're doing for enjoyment and it should be something that you and your family can do together. You don't want to push the family out of your life and make the race car the most important thing. I think it should be something that's done together. It's going to take you quite a while before you can even win a local bracket race because the people you're up against are very experienced. If you approach it with the attitude that you're going to have a good time, whether you win or lose, it will be a successful deal for you.

Some General Tips

A great many very experienced people have one common thread of advice when it comes to starting out: First, if you want to win, concentrate on improving yourself.

Concentrate, they said, on making yourself consistent. Strive to make the actual act of racing intuitive, so that when you're up at the line you can make the big stuff second nature; how you're going to stage, where you're going to do the burnout if you have the right equipment, when you'll hit the throttle and so forth.

They said also to know your car. If you've been going to one track for ten years, you really should be able to tell what the track will do when it's June and a light wind is coming out of the west and it's noon and the sun is directly overhead. At that point, all the dials and gauges shouldn't be any match for what your experience tells you. You should know intuitively what's happening. You may check the instruments to make sure you're on target, but you'd better already know it.

And most importantly, they said, race the car the same way for a while before changing it, and only then change small things, then test the effect before changing anything else. They suggested that one of the most common mistakes new racers make is to keep adjusting things just for the sake of adjusting. They feel they will run better, be faster, or whatever. In reality, changing things before you've gotten a season's worth of runs in the same car will stop you from progressing to where you wanted to go in the first place. If you start with a decent car, stay with it. Don't change things because the other guys are doing it—even if you trust their judgment. Chances are, you'll be following them off a cliff.

The second universal tip was to make sure you race against people better than you. Many new drivers are afraid of going against a guy who really knows what he's doing. It's always safer to go against an inexperienced new guy, because most likely you're going to beat the pants off him. That's wonderful for your ego, but it does little for your education. Go against the track champion. See what he does, see how he approaches the sport. Try to beat him. If you

This is what an NHRA National Event looks like from above. All you have to do is compete in three divisional races, and you can enter one of these events to run with the big boys. Are you ready?

"But you must also be realistic. You may be the best in the world, it still doesn't mean you can make a living at drag racing."

do, you've really accomplished something. If you don't you'll know what the standard is.

Life is full of mediocrity, and the best way to conquer it is to disbelieve any criticisms of yourself; to follow your heart and, if you truly want it, to go get it. But you must also be realistic. You may be the best in the world, it still doesn't mean you can make a living at drag racing.

There have been many good racers with a lot of talent who have spent entire fortunes racing and never accomplished much. These were good businessmen who made their money on their own and tried to do the same in racing. And they were eaten alive. In some cases, some very famous people lost family fortunes chasing a dream they would never achieve.

A Final Note

Drag racing, then, is not just a sport of individuals participating as a group, but a sport of individuals competing against themselves. And it is a forum for evolution. Social evolution, mechanical evolution and, most importantly, personal evolution.

How good are you? Who knows. You won't know unless you try; unless you push yourself to do things that you may very well fail at. Moving from a spectator to a participant is beyond the comfort level of most folks, and we applaud you for even picking up this book. Good luck. ■

DRAGSTRIP DIRECTORY

Reprinted courtesy Hot Rod magazine

1/8 mile, March 1-November 31
Events: FBC/Sat. nights

HOLIDAY RACEWAY
Rt. 1, Box 117
Woodstock, AL 35188
205/938-2123
1/8 mile, Mid March-October
Events: SC/Saturday nights/$15

HUNTSVILLE DRAGWAY
913 W. 16th Ave.
Birmingham, AL 35204
(In Huntsville, AL)
205/251-731
1/8 mile, March-November
Events: Heads-up Class

ALABAMA

ATMORE DRAGWAY
P.O. Box 770
Flomaton, AL 36441
(In Atmore, AL)
334/368-8363 (phone)
334/296-3200 (fax)
1/8 mile, February-October
Events: TNT/Sundays/$5
Grudge/Sundays/$5

BAILEYTON GOOD TIME DRAGSTRIP
P.O. Box 64, Baileyton, AL 35019
(In Cullman, AL)
205/796-2892

1/8 mile, April-September
Events: BR-SC/Saturday nights/$10

BAMA DRAGWAY
PO. Box 1824
Jasper, AL 35019
205/221-3342
1/8 mile, Mid March through
Mid November
Events: TNT/March/$5
SC/Saturday nights in April/$10

CHATOM INTERNATIONAL DRAGWAY
P.O. Box 530
Chatom, AL 36518
334/847-3575
334/847-2442 (fax)

AMATEUR RACING PROGRAMS—LIST OF ABBREVIATIONS

Bracket Racing	BR
Street Class	SC
ET Events	ET
Footbrake Class	FBC
Friday Night Drags	FND
Grudge Racing	Grudge
Jr. Dragsters	JR
Outlaw Street Racers	OSR
Test 'n Tune	TNT
Trophy Class	TC
Powder Puff	PP
Sears Craftsman	Sears
High School	HS

Twice monthly/Free
Grudge, TNT Thursdays/$8
FBC (no electronics)/Saturdays/$15

MOBILE INTERNATIONAL RACEWAY
P.O. Box 54
Irvington, AL 36544
334/957-2026 (phone)
334/957-2063 (fax)
1/8 mile, April-October
Events: SC/Fridays/$15

PHENIX DRAGSTRIP
P.O. Box 1691
Phenix City, AL 36867
334/291-0494
1/8 mile, Year-round
Events: TNT Tuesdays/$5
SC/Sundays/$7

ALASKA

FAIRBANKS RACING LIONS
175 E. Van Horn
Fairbanks, AK 99701
907/452-8913
1/4 mile, May-September

Events: BR-SC/Saturday
& Sunday/$40

ARIZONA

FIREBIRD INTERNATIONAL RACEWAY
Box 5023, 2000 Maricopa Rd.
Chandler, AZ 85226
1-800-DRAG-INFO
602/268-0200 (phone)
602/796-0531 (fax)
1/4 mile, Year-round
Events: FND/Fridays/$10
BR/Saturday, once a month/$10
JR Friday nights

PHOENIX RACEWAY PARK
19421 W. Jomax Rd.
Wittmann, AZ 85361
602/256-0333 (phone)
602/388-2326 (fax)
1/4 mile, Year-round
Events: BR-TC/Sat. or Sun.
bimonthly/$20
OSR/Saturday night, monthly/$15
FND-SC/Fridays/$10

ARKANSAS

NEWPORT OPTIMIST DRAGWAY
109 Main St.
Newport, AR 72112
501/523-5172 (phone)
1/8 mile, February-October
Events: TNT/Sundays in
early season/$10
TC (stock vehicles)/Sundays/$10

CALIFORNIA

CARLSBAD RACEWAY
430 Cribbage Ln. Unit C
San Marcos, CA 92069
(In Carlsbad, CA)
619/727-4390 (phone)
619/727-1171 (fax)
1/4 mile, Year-round
Events: BR-SC/Monthly
on Sunday/$25
Grudge/Saturdays/$15

FAMOSO RACEWAY
33559 Famoso Rd
McFarland, CA 93250
(In Bakersfield, CA)
805/399-2210 (phone)
805/399-2608 (fax)
1/4 mile, February-November
Events: Grudge/Fri. nights
(April-Oct.)/$10
TNT/Fri. Nights (April-Oct.)/$10
JR Saturdays (April-Sept.)/$10
Sears-ET/Sat. (April-Sept.)/$10
Fun Ford Weekend/End of April
Big Bucks BR Monthly
(April-Sept.)/$100 prize
Open testing/Monthly/$10
HS/$10

INYOKERN DRAGSTRIP
P.O. Box 182
Ridgecrest, CA 93556
(In Inyokern, CA)

619/375-8832
1/4 mile, December-May
Events: BR-Sears/Monthly/$40+
PP/Monthly/Free

LOS ANGELES
COUNTY RACEWAY
P.O. Box 901690
Palmdale, CA 93590-1690
805/533-2224 (phone)
805/533-2226 (fax)
l/4 mile, Year-round
Events: Grudge/Fridays
(March Nov.)/$10
HS/Fridays in Summer/$5
TNT/Weekly/$5

POMONA RACEWAY
2035 Financial Way
Glendora, CA 91740
(In Pomona, CA)
818/914-4761 (phone)
818/963-5360 (fax)
1/4 mile
Events: SC/Saturdays/$10

SACRAMENTO
RACEWAY PARK
5305 Excelsior Rd.
Sacramento, CA 95827
916/363-2653 (Info)
916/366-7368 (phone)
916/368-8772 (fax)
1/4 mile, Year-round
Events: BR-SC Wed. nights
(Feb-Oct.)/$10
TNT/Fri. nights (April-Oct.)/$30
TNT/Sat. nights (Nov-March)/$30

SAMOA AIRPORT
DRAGSTRIP
1822 West Ave.
Eureka, CA 95501
707/443-5203
1/4 mile, April-September
Events: BR-SC/Sundays/$15

SEARS POINT RACEWAY
Hwys. 37 and 121
Sonoma, CA 95476
707/935-7411 (phone)
707/938-8430 (fax)
1/4 mile, February-November
Events: BR Wednesday nights/$15

COLORADO

BANDIMERE SPEEDWAY
3051 S. Rooney Rd.
Morrison, CO 80465
303/697-6001 (phone)
303/697-0815 (fax)
1/4 mile, April-October
Events: TNT Wednesday nights/$25
Club Clash/Fri. Night/$20
ET/Fridays/$20
ET/Saturdays/$30
HS/Memorial & Labor Day/$25
Maximum King-SC/5 a year/$20

PUEBLO MOTORSPORTS PARK
3701 Bijou
Pueblo, CO 81008
719/545-0878
l/4 mile, April-October
Events: FND/Summer/$3
TNT/March/$10
TC/Summer/$15

DELAWARE

U.S.13
DRAGWAY
Rt. 2, Box 181
Laurel, DE 19956
(In Delmar, DE)
302/846-3968 (phone)
302/875-9083 (fax)
1/4 mile, February-November
Events: ET/Fridays & Sundays/$10
TC/Fridays & Sundays/$10

FLORIDA

DE SOTO
MEMORIAL DRAGSTRIP
21000 State Rd. 64
Bradenton, FL 34202
813/748-1320 1/4 mile, Year-round
Events: BR-SC/Saturday nights/$15
TNT Tuesdays/$10
JR Tuesdays/$10
HS Drags/Twice a season/Free

GAINESVILLE RACEWAY
1211 N. County Rd. 225
Gainesville, FL 32609
904/377-0046 (phone)
904/371-4212 (fax)
1/4 mile, Year-round
Events: TC/Saturdays/$12
TNT/Saturdays/$10
JR Saturdays/$10
Money Class/$25

JAX RACEWAYS
6840 Stuant Ave.
Jacksonville, FL 32254
904/786-7750 (phone)
904/783-6571 (fax)
1/8 mile, March-November
Events: TNT Thursdays/$15
BR-SC
Pro Super Spon/$35
Sportman Bike & St./$30

LAKELAND DRAGSTRIP
8100 Hwy. 33 N.
Lakeland, FL 33809
813/984-1145
l/8 mile, Year-round
Points races: March-October
Events: ET/Saturdays/$8
TNT Thursdays/$6

MOROSO
MOTORSPORTS PARK
P.O. Box 31907
Palm Beach Gardens, FL 33420

407/622-1400 (phone)
407/626-2053 (fax)
l/4 mile, Year-round
Events: BR/Saturday nights/$10
TNT Wednesdays & Fri. nights/$10
HS Two Saturdays a month/$10

ORLANDO SPEED WORLD DRAGWAY
P.O. Box 1097
New Smyrna Beach, FL 32170
(In Orlando, FL)
407/568-5522 (phone)
904/426-1611 (fax)
l/4 mile, April-October
Events: TNT Wednesdays/$10
Sportsmen Club/Saturdays/$10

POWER HOUSE DRAGSTRIP
300 Joan Ln.
Panama City, FL 32404
904/762-8885
1/8 mile, March-November
Events: Super ET/Saturdays/$25
TNT/Saturdays/$15

SEBRING DRAGWAY
P.O. Box 3674
Sebring, FL 33871
813/385-5095 (phone)
813/385-5095 (fax)
l/4 mile, Year-round
Events: TNT/Saturday,
twice a month/$30
Super Street Saturdays/$30

GEORGIA

ATLANTA DRAGWAY
Rt. 1, Box 142
Commerce, GA 30529
706/335-2301 (phone)
404/335-7135 (fax)
1/4 mile, March-November
Events: BR/Saturdays/$25
Grudge/Fridays/$10
TNT/Fridays/$10

HS/$25
JR $10

PARADISE DRAGWAY
500 Chatsworth Hwy. N.E
Calhoun, GA 30701
706/629-6161
1/8 mile, Year-round
Events: BR-SC/Sundays/$20
FBC/Sundays/$20

SAVANNAH DRAGSTRIP
6411 Garrard Ave.
Savannah, GA 31405
912/234-1965 (phone)
912/927-4347 (fax)
1/8 mile, February-November
Events: BR (Sportsman)/
Saturdays/$25
TNT Wednesdays/$10

SILVER DOLLAR RACEWAY
P.O. Box 512
Reynolds, GA 31076
912/847-4414
1/4 mile, Year-round
Events: TNT/Fridays
& Saturdays/$10
BR-SC/Saturdays/$15

SOUTHEASTERN INTERNATIONAL DRAGSTRIP
2337 Lake Rd
Hiram, GA 30141
(In Dallas, GA)
404/445-2183
1/8 mile, April-October
Events: BR-SC/Saturday nights/$35

SOUTHERN DRAGWAY
P.O. Box 1500
Douglas, GA 31533
912/384-7733 (phone)
912/384-6065 (fax)
1/8 mile, February-December
Events: TNT Thursdays/$15
Grudge Thursdays/$15

HAWAII

HAWAII RACEWAY PARK
94-165 Leonue St.
Waipahu, HI 96797
(In Ewa Beach, HI)
801/671-1706
(phone & fax)
1/4 mile, February-December
Events: BR/Friday, Saturday
& Sunday/$60
SC/Friday or Saturday nights/$5

MAUI RACEWAY PARK
P.O. Box 6020
Kahului, HI 96732
(In Puunene, HI)
808/878-1000
1/4 mile, February-November
Events: BR-SC/Saturdays/$10
BR/Sundays/$25

IDAHO

DRAG CITY RACEWAY
1249 S. Hwy. 30
Pocatello, ID 83252
208/766-2711
1/8 mile, April-October
Events: TNT BR/varies
HS

ILLINOIS

COLES COUNTY DRAGWAY
P.O. Box 634
Charleston, IL 61920
217/345-7777 (phone)
812/232-6115 (fax)
1/8 mile, April-October
Events: TNT/Once a month
on Sunday/$10
SC/Sundays/$15
HS/6 times a year/$15
PP/5 times a season/$15
JR (8-18 years)

GATEWAY INTERNATIONAL RACEWAY

558 N. Hwy. 203
Fairmont City, IL 62201
(In Madison, IL)
618/482-5546 (phone)
618/482-5595 (fax)
1/4 mile, March-October
Events: Wednesdays &
Saturdays/$10-$40
HS/Fridays (6-8 per season)/
$10-$20

I-57 DRAGSTRIP

6112 Hill City Rd
Benton, IL 62812
618/439-6039
1/8 mile, April-October
Events: BR-TC/Saturday nights/$10

MASON COUNTY RACEWAY

13627 4th St.
Pekin, IL 61554
(In Havana, IL)
309/543-6124 (phone)
309/348-3119 (fax)

1/8 mile, March-October
Events: SC/Sundays/$20
HS/4 times a year/$10
TNT/Sundays/$20

INDIANA

BROWN COUNTY DRAGWAY

4396 W Branstetter Rd.
Nashville, IN 47448
812/988-1505
1/8 mile, March-October
Events: TNT/Sunday/$20
TC/Sunday/$20
Pro/Sunday/$30
Super Pro Drag ($800 pay out)/$40

BUNKER HILL DRAGSTRIP

RR 1, Box 74
Bunker Hill, IN 46914
(In Kokomo, IN)
317/689-8248
1/8 mile, April-October
Events: SC/Saturday & Sunday/$15

GREATER EVANSVILLE RACEWAY

P.O. Box 40
Chandler, IN 47630
502/521-6702
1/8 mile, March 30-October 23
Events: BR (1, 2 & Trophy)/weekly
TNT/weekly
Street Car/2nd weekend &
1st of month

INDIANAPOLIS RACEWAY PARK

P.O. Box 34300
Indianapolis, IN 46234
(In Clemmont, IN)
317/293-7223 (phone)
317/291-4220 (fax)
1/4 mile, March-October
Events: HS/Sundays/$1
BR-SC/Sundays, (Mar.-Sept.)/$25
Grudge/Wednesdays
(June-Aug.)/$10

MUNCIE DRAGWAY

P.O. Box 397
Yorktown, IN 47396
(In Muncie, IN)
317/789-8470 (phone)
317/789-6831 (fax)
1/4 mile, April-October
Events: BR-SC/Saturdays/$20
TNT Wednesday night/$15
HS/Once a year/$10

OSCEOLA DRAGWAY

56328 Ash Rd.
Osceola, IN 46561
317/789-8470 (phone)
317/789-6831 (fax)
1/4 mile
Events: BR/Saturdays & Sundays
TNT Wednesdays

U.S. 41 INTERNATIONAL DRAGWAY

P.O. Box 221

Lake Village, IN 46349
219/285-2200
1/4 mile, March-November
Events: TNT Wednesdays &
Fridays/$20
Grudge Wednesdays & Fridays/$20
King of the Mountain/$35
JR/Sundays/$20-$50

IOWA

CEDAR FALLS RACEWAY
211 E. 11th St.
Cedar Falls, IA 50613
319/987-2537

HUMBOLDT
COUNTY DRAGWAY
6 1/2 First Ave. S.
Fort Dodge, IA 50501
515/332-2510
1/8 mile, May-October
Events: BR, SC
& TC/Saturdays/$20

NEW EDDYVILLE DRAGWAY
2462 Hwy. 163
Pella, IA 50219
515/969-5596
l/8 mile, April-October
Events: BR-TC/Saturdays/$15
TNT Throughout season/$10
JR

KANSAS

HEARTLAND PARK
TOPEKA
1805 S.W. 71st
Topeka, KS 66619
800/43-RACES (phone)
913/862-2016 (fax)
1/4 mile, April-October
Events: BR (Sportsmen Class)/
Sat. & Sun., monthly/$60

MID-AMERICA DRAGWAY
Attn: Dave Riverside Autobody
2121 S. Summit
Kansas City, KS 67005

316/442-1491
1/4 mile, March-November
Events: BR-SC/Sunday,
twice a month /$15
TNT/Saturday, twice a month/$15

MIDWEST RACEWAY
1895 E-175 Rd.
Lecompton, KS 66050
(In Manhattan, KS)
913/776-7223
1/8 mile, May-October
Events: BR-TC/Sat. or
Sun., bi-monthly/$15
BR-Sportsman/Saturday/ $20

KENTUCKY

BEECH BEND RACEWAY
Bradford St.
Beechmont, KY 42323
(In Bowling Green, KY)
502/782-1138
1/4 mile, March-October
Events: BR/Sunday/$15
Grudge/Friday nights/$10
Street Car Shootout
Friday nights/$10
HS/Friday nights/$10

MOUNTAIN PARK DRAGWAY
U.S. 25 N.
Berea, KY 40403
(In Clay City)
1/8 mile, March-December
Events: BR-SC/$30
No Electronics Class/Saturdays/$30
TC (1/4-mile runs)/ Saturdays/$20

OHIO VALLEY RACEWAY
3312 Gilmore Industrial
Blvd., Louisville, KY 40213
(In West Point, KY)
502/922-4152
1/8 mile, March-October
Events: BR-SC/Saturdays/$30
Grudge Wednesdays/$15

LOUISIANA

STATE CAPITOL DRAGWAY
Rt. 2, Box 61
Hallsvllle, TX 75650
(In Baton Rouge, LA)
504/627-4574
1/4 mile, February-November
Events: BP/Every
other Saturday/$10-$20
TNT/Fridays/$8

TWIN CITY DRAGWAY
525 Angus Rd.
Monroe, LA 71202
318/387-8563
1/4 mile, March-October
Events: BR-SC/Saturdays/$15

MAINE

OXFORD PLAINS SPEEDWAY
Rt. 26, Box 208
Oxford, ME 04270
207/539-8865 (phone)
207/539-8860 (fax)
l/4 mile, April-October 1
Events: BR TNT Wednesday HS

WINTERPORT DRAGWAY
295 Water St.
Ellsworth, ME 04605
(In Winterport, ME)
207/667-6134
1/8 mile, May-October
BR-SC/Sundays/$10
TNT/Sundays (early season)/$10

MARYLAND

MARYLAND
CAPITOL RACEWAY
P.O. Box 3698
Crofton, MD 21114
410/721-9879
l/4 mile
Events: BR, TNT

CECIL COUNTY DRAGWAY
1573 Theodore Rd.
Rising Sun, MD 21911
410/287-6280
l/4 mile, March-November
Events: TNT, BR, HS

MARYLAND INTERNATIONAL RACEWAY
8904 Centreville Rd.
Manassas, VA 22110
(In Budds Creek, MD)
301/884-9833 (phone)
703/631-2945 (fax)
l/4 mile, March-November
Events: TNT/Most Sundays/$30
ET-TC/Saturdays/$15
Midnight Madness-SC/Fridays/$10
Speed Shop Challenge
(Street cars only)/Once a year/$10

MASON-DIXON DRAGWAY
21344 National Pike
Boonsboro, MD 21713
(In Hagerstown, MD)
301/791-5193
1/4 mile, March-November
Events: TNT/Monthly
on Saturday/$15
Street Night Monthly/$20
BR-TC/Sundays/$15

75-80 DRAGWAY
11508-C Finger Board Rd.
Monrovia, MD 21770
301/865-5102 (phone)
301/831-3092 (fax)
1/4 mile, March-November
Events: TNT/Monthly/$15
BR-SC Twice a week/$15
HS Drags/4 per year/$15

MICHIGAN

DETROIT DRAGWAY
18458 Sumner Rd.
Redford Ml 48240

313/479-2190
1/4 mile
Events: TNT/$15

UPPER INTERNATIONAL DRAGWAY
1616 Vernor Rd.
Lapeer, Ml 48446
313/664-4772
1/4 mile, April-November
Events: BR-SC/Sundays/$15

MID MICHIGAN MOTORPLEX
2589 N. Wyman Rd.
Stanton, Ml 48888
517/762-5190 (phone)
517/831-8981 (fax)
1/4 mile, April-October
Events: BR/Saturdays
& Sundays/$40
TNT/Wednesdays/$15
Grudge/Wednesdays/ $15
TC/Saturdays & Sundays/$15

MILAN
INTERNATIONAL DRAGWAY
2609 Otter
Warren, Ml 48092
313/439-7368 (phone)
313/439-3494 (fax)
l/4 mile, April-October
Events: BPJWednesdays/$30-35
TNT Wednesdays/$15
Grudge/Fridays/$15

NORTHERN
MICHIGAN DRAGWAY
P.O. Box 19
Kaleva, Ml 49845
616/362-3439
1/8 mile, June-September
Events: BR-SC/Sundays/$25

UBLY DRAGWAY
4812 S. Ubly Rd.
Ubly, MI 48475
517/658-2331 (phone)

517/658-2331 (fax)
l/4 mile, May-October
Events: BR-SC/Sundays/$25
TNT/Saturdays/$15

MINNESOTA

BRAINERD INTERNATIONAL RACEWAY
17113 Minnetonka Blvd., #214
Minnetonka, MN 55345
(In Brainerd, MN)
218/829-9836 (phone)
612/752-2149 (fax)
l/4 mile, April-October
Events: BR-SC/Sat. and Sun.
bi-monthly/$50

MISSISSIPPI

BYHALIA RACEWAY PARK
P.O. Box 732
Fulton, MS 38843
(In Byhalia, MS)
601/838-4350
1/8 mile, March-November
Events: BR-SC/Saturdays/$25

FULTON DRAGWAY
P.O. Box 732
Fulton, MS 38843
601/862-2232
1/8 mile, March-November
Events: BR-SC/Sundays/$20

GULFPORT DRAGWAY
P.O. Box 885
Long Beach, MS 39560
(In Gulfport, MS)
601/863-4408
1/4 mile, Year-round
Events: BR-SC/
Sundays, bimonthly/$15
King of the Hill-HS/
Wednesdays/$10

NORTHEAST MISSISSIPPI MOTORSPORTS
P.O. Box 178
Aberdeen, MS 39730
601/369-6888
1/8 mile, February-October
Events: BP Saturdays/$20
TNT/Fridays/$10

MISSOURI

KANSAS INTERNATIONAL RACEWAY
17900 Cheyenne Dr.
Independence, MO 64056
(In Kansas City, MO)
816/358-6700
1/4 mile, March-November
Events: BR-SC/Saturdays/$15
Grudge/Wednesdays/$8
HS-SC/Saturday twice a year/
$15 JR

MID-AMERICA RACEWAY
1112 Hwy. T
Foristell, MO 63348
(In Wentzville, MO)
314/639-6465
1/4 mile, April-October
Events: TC/Saturday & Sunday/$15

MO-KAN DRAGWAY
1603 N. Elm St.,
Pittsburg, KS 66762
(In Ashbury, MO)
417/642-5599
1/4 mile, March-November
Events: BR/Saturdays
(Sundays in Fall)

U.S. 36 RACEWAY
Rt. 1, Box 9-A
Osborn, MO 64474
(In Cameron, MO)
816/675-2279
l/8 mile, April-October

Events: BR-SC/Saturdays/$30
Showroom Class/Saturdays/$20
TNT Wednesdays/$10

NEBRASKA

NEBRASKA MOTORPLEX
13116 Lockwood Plaza Cir.
Omaha, NE 68142-4245
(In Scribner, NE)
402/664-2577 (phone)
402/238-2774 (fax)
1/4 mile, April-October
Events: BR-SC/Sunday, 3 times a
month/$49
TNT/Sat. 2-3 times a month/$29
SC/Friday nights, twice a
month/$10
Pepsi HS Challenge/$15
JR

NEVADA

U.S. VEGAS SPEEDWAY PARK
6000 Las Vegas Blvd.
N. Las Vegas, NV 89115
702/643-3333 (phone)
702/644-0363 (fax)
l/4 mile, March-November
Events: BR-SC & HS/Sat.
(twice a mo.)/$20
TNT/Friday nights/$10

NEW HAMPSHIRE

NEW ENGLAND DRAGWAY
P.O. Box 1320 Rt. 27
Epping, NH 03042
603/679-8001 (phone)
603/679-1955 (fax)
1/4 mile, April-October
Events: TNT/Saturdays/$25
BR-ET/Sundays/$20
Cruising Drag Night/Fridays/$15
Grudge-SC/Wednesday/$12
Grudge-SC/Friday/$15

NEW JERSEY

ATCO DRAGWAY
P.O. Box 182
Atco, NJ 08004
609/768-2167 (phone)
609/753-9604 (fax)
609/768-0900 (hotline)
1/4 mile, Year-round
Events: BR Saturdays/$20
TNT/Every other Sunday/$20
SC/Tuesday & Friday/$10

ISLAND DRAGWAY
P.O. Box 184
(Off Rt. 46)
Great Meadows, NJ 07838
908/637-6060
l/4 mile, March-November
Events: BR-SC/Weekends/$25
TNT/Sat. early season,
Sun. late/$20
JR

OLD BRIDGE TOWNSHIP RACEWAY PARK
230 Pension Rd.
Englishtown, NJ 07726
908/446-6331 (phone)
908/446-1373 (fax)
1/4 mile, March-November
Events: TNT/Wednesday nights/$15
BR/Fridays/$20
HS/Once per season/$20

NEW MEXICO

ALBUQUERQUE NATIONAL DRAGWAY
1309 Eubank N.E.
Albuquerque, NM 87112
505/873-2684
1/4 mile, March-November
Events: BR-SC/Saturday or
Sunday/$27
TNT, SC/Sunday, once a month/$10

ROSWELL DRAGWAY
1602 S. Beach
Roswell, NM 88201
505/623-1988
l/4 mile, March-October
Events: BR-ET/Sunday,
a month/$39
JR

THE DRAG CLUB
P.O. Box 3643
Alamagordo, NM 88311
(In Carrizozo, NM)
505/437-3936
l/4 mile, March-November
Events: BR-SC/Every 3rd
Sunday/$35
TNT/Every 3rd Sunday/$15

NEW YORK

APPLE VALLEY SPEEDWAY
203 Milburn St.
Rochester, NY 14607
(In Williamson, NY)
315/589-2310 (phone)
315/986-3491 (fax)
1/10 mile, April-October
Events: SC/Fridays/$20

Beat Your Buddy/Weekly/
Free racing for spectators
with own cars
JR

ESTA SAFETY PARK DRAGSTRIP
2719 Lamson Rd.
Phoenix, NY 13135
(In Cicero, NY)
315/699-7484
1/4 mile, April-October
Events: BR-TC/Sundays/$15
JR/Weekly

LANCASTER SPEEDWAY
P.O. Box M
Clarence, NY 14031
(In Buffalo, NY)
716/839-0857 (phone)
716/759-681 9 (fax)
1/8 mile, April-October
Events: BR-SC/Fridays/$20
TNT/Tuesdays/$10
JR Tuesdays

LEBANON VALLEY DRAGWAY
Rt. 20
West Lebanon, NY 12195

518/794-8968
l/4 mile, April-October
Events: BR-SC/Sundays/$15
TNT/Wed. nights & Saturdays/$15

LONG ISLAND DRAGWAY
P.O. Box 423
Farmingville, NY 11738
(In Westhampton, NY)
516/288-1555
l/4 mile, March-December
Events: TC/Saturdays/$30
BR Fri., Sat. & Sun. afternoons/$25
JR/Saturdays/$25

NEW YORK INTERNATIONAL RACEWAY PARK
P.O. Box 296
Leicester, NY 14481
716/382-3030
l/4 mile, April-November
Events: BR/Saturdays/$20
BR Wednesday nights/$7
TNT/Fridays/$10

NORTH CAROLINA

BREWER'S SPEEDWAY
6728 Reedy Branch Rd.
Rocky Mount, NC 27803
919/446-2631
l/8 mile, April-November
Events: BR/Saturdays/$10
TNT/Fridays/$10
SC/Fridays, once a month/$10

COASTAL PLAINS DRAGWAY
P.O. Box 1268
Jacksonville, NC 28540
910/347-2200 (phone)
919/455-2215 (fax)
1/8 and 1/4 mile, April-November
Events: BR-SC/Saturday nights/$25
TNT/Wednesday nights/$10

DUNN-BENSON DRAGSTRIP
Rt. 1 Box 571
Dunn, NC 28334
(In Benson, NC)
l/8 mile, March-November

Events: BR/Saturdays/$8
TNT/Thursdays/$5

FARMINGTON DRAGWAY
4441 Bridle Path
Winston-Salem, NC 27103
(In Farmington, NC)
910/998-3443
1/8 mile
Events: TNT

HARRELLS RACEWAY
Rt. 1, Box 243
Willard, NC 28478
(In Harrells, NC)
910/532-2363 (phone)
919/532-4462 (fax)
l/8 mile, Year-round
Events: BR -SC/Sundays/$30
TNT/Saturdays/$10

McKENZIE RACE TRACK
Rt. 4, Box 735
Bladenboro, NC 28320
(In Hallsboro, NC)
910/648-6447
1/8 mile, Year-round
Events: BR-SC/Sundays/$25
TNT/Fridays/$5

MOORESVILLE DRAGWAY
8415 Hwy. 152 W
Mooresville, NC 28115
(In Rowan, NC)
704/664-4685
1/8 mile, April 1-October 31
Events: Reg. Spectator Race/
Sat. nights/$7
BR/Saturdays/$8-25
TNT/Friday nights/$10

NORTH WILKESBORO DRAGWAY PARK
P.O. Box 54
Grassy Creek, NC 28361
(In Wilkesboro, NC)

910/973-7223
1/8 mile
Events: BR/Saturdays
TNT/Sundays

PIEDMONT DRAGWAY
6750 Holt Store Rd.
Julian, NC 27283
910/449-7411
1/8 mile
March-December
Events: BR-SC/Sundays/$20
TNT Thursdays & Sundays/$5

ROCKINGHAM DRAGWAY
P.O. Box 70
Marston, NC 28363
(In Rockingham, NC)
910/582-3400 (phone)
910/582-8667 (fax)
1/4 mile, March-November
Events: RR-SC/Saturdays/$15
Street Drags/Fridays/$10

ROXBORO DRAGWAY
P.O. Box 2
Durham, NC 27702
910/364-3724
1/8 mile
Events: TNT/Saturdays

SHADYSIDE DRAGWAY
Rt. 8, Box 1425-B
Hickory, NC 28602
(In Boiling Springs, NC)
704/434-7313 (phone)
704/434-0930 (fax)
1/8 mile Events: TNT, BR-Pro

SHUFFLETOWN DRAGWAY
8621 Larchmont Circle
Charlotte, NC 28214
704/399-5071
1/8 mile, March-October
Events: BR/Sundays
TNT/Saturdays
HS/Monthly

WIIKESBORO DRAGWAY PARK
P.O. Box 54
Grassy Creek, NC 28631
(In Wilkesboro, NC)
910/973-7223
1/8 mile, March-November
Events:
BR Friday & Saturday/$25
TNT/Friday & Saturday/$10

OHIO

BRUSH RUN PARK
67160 Airport Rd.
St. Clairsville, OH 43950
614/695-0908
1/8 mile, May-October
Event: TNT/1st Sun. each month/
$2 per run

DRAGWAY 42
P.O. Box 816
West Salem, OH 44287
419/853-4242 (phone)
419/853-4083 (fax)
1/4 mile, March-November
Events: SC/Sundays/$8
TNT/Wednesdays/$8

EDGEWATER SPORTS PARK
4819 Miami River Rd.
Cleves, OH 45002
(In Cincinnati)
513/353-4666 (phone)
513/353-1608 (fax)
1/4 mile, March-November
Events: BR-TC/Saturday
 or Sunday/$15
TNT/Fridays/$10

K.D. DRAGWAY
1192 State Rd. 140
South Webster, OH 45682
614/778-2453 (phone)
614/778-2594 (fax)
1/8 mile, April-November
Events: BR/Saturdays/$25

TNT/Fridays/$15
TC/Fridays/$15
FB/Fridays/$15

MARION COUNTY INTERNATIONAL RACEWAY
2454 Richwood-LaRue Rd.
LaRue, OH 43332
614/499-3666 (phone)
614/499-2185 (fax)
1/4 mile, April-October
Events: BR-SC/Saturdays/$20
TNT/Fridays/$15
TC/Fridays/$15

NATIONAL TRAIL RACEWAY
2650 National Rd. SW
Hebron, OH 43025-9798
614/928-5706 (phone)
614/928-2922 (fax)
1/4 mile, April-November
Events: BR, TNT, Grudge/
Sundays, April-Nov. 17 &
Wednesdays, May 1-Sept. 25

NORWALK RACEWAY PARK
1300 State Rt. 18
Norwalk, OH 44857
419/668-5555 (phone)
419/663-0502 (fax)
1/4 mile, April-October
Events: BR-SC & TC/
Saturdays/$10
TNT/Fridays/$10

QUAKER CITY DRAGWAY
10359 S. Range Rd.
Salem, OH 44460
216/332-5335 (phone)
216/332-9300 (fax)
1/4 mile, April-September
Events: BR-SC/Sundays/$10
HS-SC/Sundays/$10
TNT/Wednesdays $5
Jr. Dragsters

TRI-STATE DRAGWAY
P.O. Box 283
Ross, OH 45061
(In Hamilton, OH)
513/863-0562
1/4 mile, March-October
Events: BR-SC & TC/Sundays/$15
TNT/Saturday early season
Thursday late season/$10

OKLAHOMA

ARDMORE RACEWAY
P.O. Box 141
Springer, OK 73458
(In Ardmore, OK)
405/653-2711
1/4 mile, March-October
Events: SC/Saturday & Sunday/$30

THUNDER VALLEY RACEWAY PARK
P.O. Box 617
Noble, OK 73068
405/872-3420 (phone)
405/872-9725 (fax)
l/4 mile, February-November
Events: BR-SC/Saturdays/$20
TNT/Fridays/$12
HS/Fridays/$12

OREGON

COOS BAY INTERNATIONAL SPEEDWAY
P. O. Box 1559
Coos Bay, OR 97420
503/269-2474
1/8 mile, April-October
Events: BR-SC/Bi-Monthly
on Sunday
TNT/End of April
JR/Free

PORTLAND INTERNATIONAL RACEWAY
1940 N. Victory Blvd.

Portland, OR 97217
503/285-6635 (phone)
503/285-0363 (fax)
1/8 and 1/4 mile, February-October
Events: BR-SC & TC/Sunday
early season; Wednesday
late season/$12
HS/May 12
JR

WOODBURN DRAGSTRIP
7730 Hwy. 219
Woodburn, OR 97071
503/982-4461
l/4 mile, March-October
Events: BR-SC/Sundays/$25
TNT/Saturdays, early season/$20
HS/6 per year/$15

PENNSYLVANIA

BEAVER SPRINGS DRAGWAY
500 Summit Dr.
Lewistown, PA 17044
(In Beaver Springs, PA)
717/658-9601
1/4 mile, March-October
Events: BR-TC/Saturdays/$15
Super Street/Friday nights/$15
SC/Friday nights/$15

MAPLE GROVE RACEWAY
RD 3, Box 3420
Mohnton, PA 19540-9202
215/856-7812 (phone)
215/856-1601 (fax)
1/4 mile, April-October
Events: BR-SC/Sundays
BR-TC/Sundays/$15
TNT/Sat., early season; Fri., mid
JR

NUMIDIA RACEWAY
48 Mill St.
New Buffalo, PA 17069
(In Bloomsburg, PA)
717/799-0480

1/4 mile, Mid April-Mid October
Events: BR, TNT & Grudge/
Sundays

SOUTH MOUNTAIN DRAGWAY
RD 1 Box 204
East Berlin, PA 17316
(In Boiling Springs, PA)
717/258-6287 (phone)
717/986-1800 (fax)
l/8 mile, April-October
Events: BR-TC/Sundays/$20
Ladies Challenge/Monthly/$20
HS Drags/4 per year/$20

SOUTH CAROLINA

CAROLINA DRAGWAY
P. O. Box 1032
Jackson, SC 29831
803/471-2285 (phone)
803/471-9146 (fax)
1/4 mile, Year-round
Events: BR-SC/Weekends,
twice a month/$15
TNT/Thursdays (Feb.-Nov.)/$8
Grudge/Thursdays/$8

FLORENCE-DARLINGTON DRAGSTRIP
Rt. 3, Box 71
Florence, SC 29505
803/395-0815
18 mile, March-November
Events: BR-SC/Saturdays/$20
TNT/Sundays/$10
Grudge/Sundays/$10
TC/Sundays/$10

GREER DRAGWAY
1477 Hwy. 357
Lyman, SC 29365
(In Greer, SC)
803/879-4634 (phone)
803/877-0457 (fax)
l/8 mile, Mid February-November
Events: BR/Saturdays/$10

TNT Thursdays/$5
Spectators/$7

ORANGEBURG DRAGSTRIP

125 Douchlee Lane
Columbia, SC 29223
(In Orangeburg, SC)
803/534-3428
1/8 mile, February-December
Events: BR-SC/6-8 per year/$25
TNT Thursdays/$5

SOUTH DAKOTA

STURGIS DRAGWAY

817 Tilford St.
Sturgis, SD 57785
605/347-4804 (phone)
605/347-3571 (fax)
l/8 mile, May-October
Events: BR $36

TENNESSEE

BRISTOL INTERNATIONAL RACEWAY

P.O. Box 729
Morehead, KY 40351
(In Bristol, TN)
615/764-3724 (phone)
606/784-4520 (fax)
1/4 mile, April-November
Events: BR-SC/Saturdays &
Sundays/$15
TNT/Fridays/$5
JR

CLARKSVILLE SPEEDWAY

923 Commerce St.
Clarksville, TN 37040
615/645-2523 (phone)
615/552-0975 (fax)
1/8 mile, March-September
Events: BR -SC/Fridays/$20
TNT/Wednesdays/$10

ENGLISH MOUNTAIN DRAGWAY

126 Kilby St.
Sevierville, TN 37862
(In Newport, TN)
615/625-8375
1/8 mile
Events: BR/Saturdays/$10-$30
TNT/Fridays & Saturdays/$10

FOUR ELEVEN (411) MOTOR SPEEDWAY

P.O. Box 370
Alcoa, TN 37701
(In Knoxville, TN)
615/573-5031 (phone)
615/984-0155 (fax)
1/8 mile, February-November
Events: BR/Saturday

JACKSON DRAGWAY

22 Barfield Cove
Jackson, TN 38305
901/423-9784
1/8 mile, March-November
Events: BR-SC/Saturdays/$25

BR-TC/Saturdays/$15
TNT/Fridays/$10

KNOXVILLE DRAGWAY

4119 N. Broadway
Knoxville, TN 37917
615/992-5000 (phone)
615/689-5528 (fax)
1/8 mile, March-October
Events: BR-FBC/Saturdays/$25
TNT/Fridays/$12
JR

MEMPHIS MOTORSPORTS PARK

5500 Taylor Forge Rd.
Millington, TN 38053
901/358-7223
1/8 & 1/4 mile, March-October

MIDDLE TENNESSEE DRAGWAY

14496 Nashville Hwy.
Buffalo Valley, TN 38548
(In Cookeville, TN)
615/858-2912

1/8 mile, March-October
Events: BR-TC/Sundays
early & late season;
Friday nights, mid-season/$10

MUSIC CITY RACEWAY
3302 Ivy Point Rd.
Goodlettsville, TN 37072
(In Nashville, TN)
615/876-0981
1/8 mile, March-October
Events: BR-SC/Saturdays/$15
SC/Friday nights/$10
Grudge/Friday nights/$10
HS/Friday nights/$10
JR/Friday nights

U.S. 43 DRAG RACEWAY
103 Dunn Rd.
Leoma, TN 38468
(In Lawrenceburg, TN)
615/762-4596
1/8 mile, April-November
Event: BR/Saturdays
TNT/Fridays

TEXAS

ALAMO DRAGWAY
107 Vincent
San Antonio, TX 78211
210/628-1872 (phone)
210/922-2580 (fax)
1/4 mile, Year-round
Events: BR-SC/Saturdays/$15
TNT Wednesday nights/$10
HS/Fridays,
three times a season/$10

AMARILLO DRAGWAY
P.O. Box 821371
Ft. Worth, TX 76182
(In Amarillo, TX)
806/622-2010 (phone)
817/498-8463 (fax)
1/4 mile, March-November
Events: BR-SC/Sundays/$10

TNT/Fridays every other week $5

CEDAR CREEK DRAGWAY
2335 Cartwright
Dallas, TX 75212
(In Aley, TX)
903/498-8643
1/8 mile, Year-round
Events: BR Saturdays/$15
TNT/Fridays & Sundays/$15

HALLSVILLE. RACEWAY
Rt. 2, Box 61
Hallsville, TX 75650
(In Longview, TX)
903/668-2858 (phone)
903/668-1724 (fax)
1/4 mile, Year-round
Events: BR-SC/Sundays/$25
TNT/Fridays & Sundays/$8

HOUSTON RACEWAY PARK
P.O. Box 1345
Baytown, TX 77522
713/383-2666 (phone)
713/383-3777 (fax)
1/4 mile, January-November
Events: Street Tire/Saturdays/$20
Street Tire Wednesdays/$12
Grudge/Fridays/$15
HS/Saturdays/$15

PENWELL RACEWAY
P.O. Box 12925
Odessa, TX 79768
915/362-2241
1/4 mile, February-October
Events: BR-SC/Sunday,
once a month/$14

TEMPLE
ACADEMY DRAGWAY
Rt. 1, Box 191
Holland, TX 76534
(In Little River, TX)
817/982-4512 (phone)
817/982-0019 (fax)

1/8 mile, February-December
Events: BR/Saturday & Sunday/$40
TNT/Saturday & Sunday/$10

TEXAS MOTORPLEX
P.O. Box 1439
Ennis, TX 75120
214/875-2641 (phone)
214/875-1848 (fax)
1/4 mile, February-November
Events: TNT/Saturdays/$20
SC/Fridays/$12
HS/Saturdays/$10

TEXAS RACEWAY
P.O. Box 262
Kennedale, TX 76060
(In Fort Worth, TX)
817/483-8410 (phone)
817/483-0610 (fax)
1/8 mile, February-November
Events: BR-SC/Saturdays/$20
HS/Once a year/$20
TNT Wednesdays/$15
SC/Fridays/$12

ST. GEORGE RACEWAY PARK
446 Rocco Rd.
Washington, UT 84780
(In St. George, UT)
801/635-2447
1/4 mile, March-November
Events: BR-TC/Bimonthly on
Saturday/$20
TNT/March

VIRGINIA

COLONIAL BEACH DRAGWAY
306-A Industrial Ct.
Leesburg, VA 22075
(In Colonial Beach, VA)
804/224-7455
1/8 mile, March-November
Events: BR-SC/Sundays/$20
TNT/Fridays/$10

EASTSIDE DRAGWAY
Rt. 340
Waynesboro, VA
703/943-9336
l/8 mile
Events: BR/Fridays & Sundays/$15

ELK CREEK DRAGWAY
Rt. 2, Box 297
Pulaski, VA 24301
(In Elk Creek, VA)
703/674-4161
1/8 mile, March-October
Events: BR-SC/Saturdays/$10
TNT/Fridays/$10

OLD DOMINION SPEEDWAY
10611 Dumfries Rd.
Manassas, VA 22111
703/361-7223
l/8 mile, March-October
Events: BR-SC/Fridays &
Sundays/$15

NEW LONDON DRAGWAY
Rt. 811
Forrest, VA
804/525-3650
l/8 mile
Events: BR/Sundays/$15

WASHINGTON

BREMERTON RACEWAY
Ted Newmille
4516 S. 10th
Tacoma, WA 98405
206/752-5917 (phone)
206/895-3616 (fax)
l/4 mile, March-October
Events: BR-SC/Every other week
$18
TNT/5 or 6 a season/$15
HS/Biweekly at every BR
event/$13

SEATTLE INTERNATIONAL RACEWAY
31001 144th Ave. S.E.
Kent, WA 98042
206/631-1550 (phone)
206/630-0888 (fax)
l/4 mile, April-November
Events: BR-SC/Friday & Saturday
nights/$20
TNT Wednesdays/$20

SPOKANE RACEWAY PARK
101 N. Hayford Rd.
Spokane, WA 99204
509/244 3663 (phone)
509/244-2472 (fax)
l/4 mile 1st Sunday in April
2nd Sunday in October
Events: BR-TC &
Money/Saturdays/$17
TNT/Friday nights/$7
HS/Friday nights/$7

WEST VIRGINIA

FAIRMONT DRAGWAY
Rt. 2, Box 511
Bridgeport, WV 26330
(In Fairmont, WV)
304/534-5381
l/8 mile, April-October
Events: BP Saturdays/$20
HS/Once a month/$15
TNT Twice a week $5

WISCONSIN

GREAT LAKES DRAGWAY
18411 First St.
Union Grove, WI 53182
414/878-3783 (phone)
414/878-4462 (fax)
1/4 mile, April-October
Events: BR-SC/Saturdays
& Sundays/$25
Fun Racing, Tues., Wed. and Fri./$20
HS/Fridays once a month/$20

ROCK FALLS RACEWAY
P.O. Box 326
Elk Mound, MN 54739
(In Eau Claire, WI)
715/875-4233 (phone)
715/879-5089 (fax)
1/4 mile, April-October
Events: BR/Bimonthly
on Sunday/$25
TNT/Bimonthly on Saturdays
 prior to BR/$85
Musclecar Days/3 a season/$30

WISCONSIN INTERNATIONAL RACEWAY
W. 1460 County Trunk KK
Kaukauna, WI 54130
414/766-5577 (phone)
414/766-5738 (fax)
1/4 & l/8 mile, Mid-April through
Mid-October
Events: BR-SC, BR-Pro, BR-ET
TNT/$10

WYOMING

DOUGLAS INTERNATIONAL RACEWAY
John Kunckel
3841 Plateau PL.
Casper, WY 82604
(In Douglas, WY)
307/358-2347
l/4 mile, April-September
Events: BR-SC & BR-TC/
Sat. & Sun., Bimonthly/$30
HS/Sat. & Sun., Bimonthly/$20
JR/$20
HR

INDEX

ABOUT THE AUTHOR

Born in Mexico City of Greek and French/Scottish parents, Tony Sakkis has been covering motorsports since 1984. He spent three years as San Francisco Chronicle's motorsports writer and five seasons as the San Francisco *Examiner's* Motorsports Editor. He is also a contributor to various magazines such as *Autoweek, Prancing Horse* and *Sports Car.* A graduate of UC Berkeley, the long-time Californian has written nine books on motorsport and two novels (written under a pseudonym). He won an award for Outstanding Journalism from the Motoring Press Association and has been published in Dutch and Japanese. He now makes his home in Houston, where he writes motorsports for the Houston *Chronicle* as well as a syndicated column which appears in nearly 105 newspapers nationwide. He is married with two children. Aptly, he met his wife in the press room of a Grand Prix race. ∎

HANDBOOKS

Auto Electrical Handbook: 0-89586-238-7
Auto Upholstery & Interiors: 1-55788-265-7
Brake Handbook: 0-89586-232-8
Car Builder's Handbook: 1-55788-278-9
Street Rodder's Handbook: 0-89586-369-3
Turbo Hydra-matic 350 Handbook: 0-89586-051-1
Welder's Handbook: 1-55788-264-9

BODYWORK & PAINTING

Automotive Detailing: 1-55788-288-6
Automotive Paint Handbook: 1-55788-291-6
Fiberglass & Composite Materials: 1-55788-239-8
Metal Fabricator's Handbook: 0-89586-870-9
Paint & Body Handbook: 1-55788-082-4
Sheet Metal Handbook: 0-89586-757-5

INDUCTION

Holley 4150: 0-89586-047-3
Holley Carburetors, Manifolds & Fuel Injection: 1-55788-052-2
Rochester Carburetors: 0-89586-301-4
Turbochargers: 0-89586-135-6
Weber Carburetors: 0-89586-377-4

PERFORMANCE

Aerodynamics For Racing & Performance Cars: 1-55788-267-3
Baja Bugs & Buggies: 0-89586-186-0
Big-Block Chevy Performance: 1-55788-216-9
Big Block Mopar Performance: 1-55788-302-5
Bracket Racing: 1-55788-266-5
Brake Systems: 1-55788-281-9
Camaro Performance: 1-55788-057-3
Chassis Engineering: 1-55788-055-7
Chevrolet Power: 1-55788-087-5
Ford Windsor Small-Block Performance: 1-55788-323-8
Honda/Acura Performance: 1-55788-324-6
High Performance Hardware: 1-55788-304-1
How to Build Tri-Five Chevy Trucks ('55-'57): 1-55788-285-1
How to Hot Rod Big-Block Chevys:0-912656-04-2
How to Hot Rod Small-Block Chevys:0-912656-06-9
How to Hot Rod Small-Block Mopar Engines: 0-89586-479-7
How to Hot Rod VW Engines:0-912656-03-4
How to Make Your Car Handle:0-912656-46-8
John Lingenfelter: Modifying Small-Block Chevy: 1-55788-238-X
Mustang 5.0 Projects: 1-55788-275-4

Mustang Performance ('79–'93): 1-55788-193-6
Mustang Performance 2 ('79–'93): 1-55788-202-9
1001 High Performance Tech Tips: 1-55788-199-5
Performance Ignition Systems: 1-55788-306-8
Performance Wheels & Tires: 1-55788-286-X
Race Car Engineering & Mechanics: 1-55788-064-6
Small-Block Chevy Performance: 1-55788-253-3

ENGINE REBUILDING

Engine Builder's Handbook: 1-55788-245-2
Rebuild Air-Cooled VW Engines: 0-89586-225-5
Rebuild Big-Block Chevy Engines: 0-89586-175-5
Rebuild Big-Block Ford Engines: 0-89586-070-8
Rebuild Big-Block Mopar Engines: 1-55788-190-1
Rebuild Ford V-8 Engines: 0-89586-036-8
Rebuild Small-Block Chevy Engines: 1-55788-029-8
Rebuild Small-Block Ford Engines:0-912656-89-1
Rebuild Small-Block Mopar Engines: 0-89586-128-3

RESTORATION, MAINTENANCE, REPAIR

Camaro Owner's Handbook ('67–'81): 1-55788-301-7
Camaro Restoration Handbook ('67–'81): 0-89586-375-8
Classic Car Restorer's Handbook: 1-55788-194-4
Corvette Weekend Projects ('68–'82): 1-55788-218-5
Mustang Restoration Handbook('64 1/2–'70): 0-89586-402-9
Mustang Weekend Projects ('64–'67): 1-55788-230-4
Mustang Weekend Projects 2 ('68–'70): 1-55788-256-8
Tri-Five Chevy Owner's ('55–'57): 1-55788-285-1

GENERAL REFERENCE

Auto Math:1-55788-020-4
Fabulous Funny Cars: 1-55788-069-7
Guide to GM Muscle Cars: 1-55788-003-4
Stock Cars!: 1-55788-308-4

MARINE

Big-Block Chevy Marine Performance: 1-55788-297-5

HPBOOKS ARE AVAILABLE AT BOOK AND SPECIALTY RETAILERS OR TO ORDER CALL: 1-800-788-6262, ext. 1

HPBooks
A division of Penguin Putnam Inc.
375 Hudson Street
New York, NY 10014